I0393492

CCRCs

Find the Right
Continuing Care Retirement Community (CCRC)
for Yourself or a Loved One

Ruth Alvarez

**A realistic guide from a retired real estate
agent and CCRC resident**

Fourth edition

Contents

Is The Time Right?

The worst mistake is waiting too long

Ted finally faced the fact that his wife, Abby, was in the early stages of Alzheimer's disease. His family doctor prescribed some medicines to help slow her debilitation, but Ted realized he was going to need help as Abby's condition worsened, and the aging process slowed him down.

He sold their home and moved to the city where his daughter lived with the assumption that she would help him take care of Abby. Bad assumption. His daughter made it clear she had her own family and a full-time job and could not be the support he expected.

Ted couldn't find a CCRC where he wanted to live that could accommodate both. Abby's condition and the fact that she had started to wander away limited their choices to CCRCs that had secured wings for dementia patients. Ted is now going through their savings paying for in-home caregivers.

Ted's story is real. Assuming your relatives are going to take care of you when you get old is a sweet, romantic notion that may have been true 30 years ago but is unlikely to be the case today.

Sometimes family members do care for an elderly family member, but sometimes they do a better job of running through the elderly person's savings than they do of providing long-term care.

By law, a resident must be at least 62 years old, although most CCRCs or life plan communities allow a couple to move in if at least one member is 62.

I think the late 70s or early 80s is an excellent time to move. You're likely to be healthy enough to both pass the community's health check and to engage in activities to make lifelong friends.

You're also old enough to see the beginnings of age-related problems (those aching knees or hips) that make living and maintaining your own house a challenge for the future.

The unhappy people are those who wait until they need assisted living or skilled nursing home care. They don't know anyone in their new community and often aren't able to do things to make many new friends.

After all, do you visit strangers in a nursing home? The rule of thumb is no one moves voluntarily after age 85.

The worst thing you can do for your spouse is to make them cope with moving to a CCRC after your death. Losing a spouse, selling a home and moving to a new place are stressful events for anyone to go through alone.

If you are retired or near-retirement and believe a CCRC could be the solution to your aging, you should move while you are still independent and able to take care of yourself.

Four Things to Know about Yourself

Please answer these four questions before you spend time and money looking for a CCRC and consider one suggestion.

1. Where do you want to live?

We need more than "I don't want any more snow and ice." Arizona's hot, dry climate may sound great but will you be happy there if your only child and grandchildren are in western Pennsylvania?

On the other hand, I've plenty of clients who moved to be closer to their children only to learn their children couldn't care less.

A friend moved to a beautiful new complex in Colorado where there's a ton of snow every year. She enjoys watching the maintenance crew shoveling it while she walks in shorts and a T-shirt through the enclosed walkway to the dining room or wellness center.

When she needs to go shopping or to a doctor, she takes the community bus. She wouldn't live anywhere else.

How important is climate to you? If you suffer from certain allergies or have arthritis or other diseases, there may be certain climates that are better for you than others.

It's worthwhile to check your intended location at **https://riskfactor.com**. That site is run by the nonprofit First Street Foundation and shows risks of flood, fire, air quality, and heat.

If you want to know if your community is in an official flood zone, visit **https://msc.fema.gov/portal/home**. You'll need to use this cheat sheet to decipher the results: **how-to-read-flood-insurance-rate-map-tutorial.pdf (fema.gov)**.

How close are you to emergency medical facilities and how close are you to top-rated cancer, orthopedics and heart facilities? What a blessing to be within a short drive of a place like the Mayo Clinic if you have, or your spouse has, a serious or unusual illness.

Be sure to consider the cost of living and which states will tax your retirement income (and which don't).

One of the most common mistakes I see is people from metropolitan areas moving to small cities. They think they'll enjoy being away from traffic, crime, and congestion. They do but they also miss all the educational, cultural, entertainment and free activities that larger cities offer.

Some communities have residents primarily from the surrounding area. That may lead to a prevailing culture that doesn't suit someone from a different part of the country as well as a cliquishness that may make someone feel they're back in high school.

On the other hand, I see communities in Florida where the majority of residents are from New York, New Jersey and Pennsylvania, and they have created mini-urban lifestyles there.

Think about what you really want to do with your spare time. Some older communities built around golf courses are falling on hard times as baby boomers are not such ardent duffers as past generations.

What is important to you?

2. What style of housing do you want?

You may be in an apartment/condominium type of building.

If you're going into independent living, you have choices. Many of the older communities are high rises or mid rises with apartment-style living.

They may be beautiful and expensive, but you are surrounded by people, and neighbors can be noisy. If you want a single-family home, cottage, duplex or triplex, they are out there.

Many older communities do not have garages, and cars may sit outside unprotected or under a string of open carports. Insisting on an attached garage will limit your choices, so decide now how important that is to you.

Typically, older communities also do not provide washers and dryers in their units but may have outlets.

Some communities have laundry rooms in a communal area but offer free laundry services. Would that make up for the lack of personal units?

If you want to take your dog or cat with you, you'll limit your choices to pet-friendly places. Some CCRCs do not allow pets at all or only indoor cats.

Ask if the assisted living facility allows pets. Some do nowadays. It's nice to bring your best friend with you but will you be able to care and maintain him in a year or so?

It's heartbreaking when the assisted living social worker has to tell someone the pet has to go because no one is taking care of him.

How much better if you get him adopted before you go into assisted living.

3. Can you live by the rules?

If you've lived on military bases or in a community with a strict Home Owners Association (HOA), you know what to expect and whether you can tolerate these types of rules.

If you've always lived in a single family home without an HOA, you may be amazed at how restrictive life in a CCRC can be.

Although you've paid a significant entry fee, that does not give you rights to determine how the community is run. Some executive directors appear to consider residents pesky annoyances to be marginalized as quickly as possible. (Please read the Governance chapter.)

You can come and go as you please, but you do not own the unit you live in and if you want to redecorate or remodel the unit, you may need permission from the CCRC.

The range of rules may astound you. I've seen some CCRCs that don't allow residents to use candles; some don't allow you to plant anything in whatever yard you may have; one didn't allow wind chimes on porches.

Even in the pet friendly CCRCs, expect many rules regarding your dog and expect some sniping from older residents who will loudly complain at the first bark.

You won't feel like a prisoner, but you are giving up some degree of freedom for the sake of community living. Be sure you can live with that before you sign a contract.

4. Can you live surrounded by older people?

It's wonderful to have the opportunity to make so many friends among people in your own age group.

You understand one another, and you can build a strong support system among people having the same kind of problems you do.

The drawback is that you will continually face the consequences of an aging circle of friends. That lovely couple you enjoyed playing cards with? The man had a stroke last week and is now in the nursing wing. That nice lady who always made brownies on Bunco night? She died in her sleep.

That may sound morbid, but living in a CCRC means you'll get used to the sound and sight of ambulances and emergency personnel. Your friends will age, become infirm and die. It will never stop.

If the community has only one dining room, you may find that 80% of the diners have walkers. You may be seated with people who hardly seem to know where they are or can barely feed themselves. Could you cope?

If you have come to terms with your own aging and mortality, you should be able to handle this aspect of CCRC life. If you haven't, you could find yourself isolated and depressed.

A suggestion

Don't be afraid to rent for a while. Some CCRCs offer month-to-month rentals for up to six months, and this can be a good interim step between committing to a permanent new residence and paying a large entrance fee.

I personally love living in Florida, but the heat and humidity doesn't appeal to everyone.

Don't move 1,000 miles to an area you only think you will like. Rent there a year, whether at the CCRC or not, and visit all the nearby CCRCs before you decide on your permanent location.

Bottomline

If you don't know yourself, buying into a CCRC is an expensive way to find out.

Four Types of Care

Continuing care retirement communities (CCRCs), also known as Life Plan Communities, are retirement communities with independent living, assisted living, and skilled nursing home care which often includes memory care.

A person can spend the rest of his life, or 'age in place,' in a CCRC by moving among levels of care as needed.

Independent living

Residents live in apartments, duplexes or triplexes, cottages or homes and maintain active lifestyles.

All maintenance is taken care of, and you're free to travel and live as you will.

Many residents eventually leave detached houses or duplexes for apartment living, which offers more amenities such as meals and housekeeping, but are still considered independent living.

There are rules similar to rental units on having guests and redecorating your space. Expect limitations on how long someone can stay at your unit especially if they are minors.

There should be a range of activities and wellness events offered. Some CCRCs even have doctors and dentists visit the site and most have resident chaplains.

The range of services and activities is as wide and varied as are the entrance and monthly fees.

Assisted living (AL)

Residents live in apartment like homes but receive assistance in the Activities of Daily Living (ADL) such as personal hygiene and grooming; dressing and undressing; feeding; functional transfers such as getting in and out of bed or a wheelchair; and bowel and bladder management.

Only a few CCRCs will allow someone in a wheelchair to live in independent living.

Some will require a wheelchair user to live in assisted living (assuming no other problems exist), while others will require transfer to the nursing facility.

The facility will have its own guidelines of who can be in assisted living versus a nursing facility. For instance, a common benchmark is the ability to get unaided to a designated point in the building or grounds in the event of an emergency.

The problem with assisted living is that there is no generally recognized definition of what it is, and states that regulate these facilities have different requirements for an AL license.

For this type of care, more is not necessarily better. Some families want to dump infirm seniors in assisted living because it's cheaper than a nursing facility and sounds more acceptable to the senior or their family members.

Some assisted living centers accept residents who clearly should not be there because they need the cash flow.

Some states are allowing more flexibility in care levels that are now allowed in AL.

Almost no assisted living facilities offer 24/7 medical or nursing support. At most there will be an RN (registered nurse) or LPN (licensed practical nurse) on duty Monday through Friday during normal business hours and on call for emergencies.

That can be fine for people who truly can benefit from assisted living: seniors who are mentally sharp but need some physical help with specific activities.

Seniors who would otherwise be isolated and lonely can find companionship and support. That was what AL was designed to accomplish.

Assisted living, however, was not designed or intended for the infirm.

Skilled nursing facility (SNF) (a Medicare term)

An SNF meets the criteria for accreditation required for Medicaid and Medicare reimbursement for skilled nursing care.

Residents typically require ventilator services, intravenous medications, skilled health monitoring and other nursing care services including rehabilitation.

The law requires, among other things, that every patient be under the supervision of a physician, that a physician be available on an emergency basis, that records of the condition and care of every patient be maintained, that nursing service be available 24 hours a day, and that at least one full-time registered nurse be employed.

As you can imagine, this is the most expensive level of care. A 2021 survey from Genworth Financial, a major financial services and insurance company determined the median monthly cost in an SNF was $7,908 for a semi-private room (Medicaid will not pay for private rooms) and $9,034 for a private room. By contrast, the median monthly cost for AL was $4,500.

Nursing homes today are split into two main types of care: short term rehabilitation and long-term care.

We'll discuss SNFs in another chapter but don't, as too many prospective residents do, decline to visit the SNF portion of the CCRC.

Fortunately, only about 25% of seniors currently live in SNFs. Many, many seniors, however, will suffer some type of accident, surgery or illness that requires short term rehabilitation.

Life will be so much easier for you, your family and friends if your rehabilitation can be accomplished within your retirement community.

Make sure the CCRC can offer physical therapy and rehabilitation on site.

Memory care

This is the most recent level of care at CCRCs. Residents with some degree of dementia usually were moved into the nursing facility but now may have a dedicated unit within or separate from the nursing unit.

Memory care should have a controlled and locked entry and exit section or building of the CCRC so residents can't wander away.

Activities are targeted at people with cognitive issues.

SNFs, on the other hand, have a range of medical and physical resident conditions under its roof.

Virtual CCRC in Your Own Home

Virtual CCRC is CCRC care in your own home. It's a marketing product, sometimes referred to as a CCRC without walls, designed to appeal to seniors who want to remain in their own homes as long as possible or those who'd like to move into a CCRC but don't have the funds for the entrance fee.

This only works if a CCRC is located close enough to your home so that your participation makes financial sense for the CCRC and for you.

The benefit to the CCRC is that it avoids the huge capital outlays for buildings and facilities. That's especially helpful when the economy is weak, and many seniors are unable to sell their homes to pay entrance fees.

You can receive nursing care, house cleaning, transportation, shopping and walking assistance or meal preparation. Just about any service can be provided. You also can participate in social, educational and wellness activities offered at the CCRC.

There is usually an entrance fee, monthly fee and a bundle of services that the member receives. Where you typically pay a $100,000 to $300,000 entrance fee for a residential CCRC, you might pay $20,000 to $70,000 for a CCRC without walls. Monthly fees typically range from $300 to $1000 depending on the desired level of care.

Be sure to find out if you would be given a discount and/or priority placement if you later want to enter the residential CCRC.

If you are no longer able to live independently, your contract probably provides either for your eviction or placement in assisted living.

Most plans provide for some type of refund in that case. Read the contract carefully.

A virtual CCRC is a major benefit if you have an accident or sudden illness. The plan will have a 'case manager' or equivalent who will ensure that you are taken to the proper treatment facilities and arrange all post-hospital care including therapy. That's a nice benefit for those who live alone.

The ideal candidates for virtual CCRCs are middle to upper income seniors who want to live at home but participate in the social activities offered by a nearby CCRC.

This type of plan, however, is only available for independent seniors.

Typically, the resident must be at least 60 years old, live in the service area (usually about a 30-mile radius from the CCRC facility), complete a financial and physical assessment and be free from any neurological or degenerative conditions.

This concept has not taken off the way its developers thought it would. It reminds me of prepaid legal services with the same marketing problem. It only makes financial sense for the CCRC if it charges a monthly fee, but potential customers aren't sure they will take advantage of enough services to make it worthwhile.

Virtual CCRCs compete in health care services with local or franchised senior care services (such as Home Instead, Visiting Angels or Comfort

Keepers) that allow a customer to pay and use them as needed without any contracts or commitments.

They compete in social services with churches, nonprofit and community senior centers that offer flexibility to use, drop and transfer as it suits the customer.

The virtual CCRC model has potential, but no one has really broken the code yet.

Here are the ones I know:

Arizona – **Beatitudes Campus in Phoenix** at http://www.beatitudescampus.org/health-services/home-care/

California - **Eskaton in Fair Oaks at http://www.eskaton.org/home-support-programs.html#lwh;**

Connecticut - **Seabury at Home in Bloomfield at http://www.seaburyathome.org/**;

Florida - **Shell Point, Ft. Myers at http://www.shellpoint.org/home_care.html**;

Kansas – **Brewster Place in Topeka at http://www.brewsterliving.org/Services/BrewsterConnect;**

Michigan - **Evangelical Homes of Michigan in Ann Arbor at http://www.evangelicalhomes.org/InHomeServices.aspx;**

North Carolina – **United Church Homes and Services in Newton at http://www.uchas.org/home-community-based-services.php;**

New Jersey - **Cadbury at Home in Cherry Hill at http://cadbury.org/athome/retirement/home;**

Pennsylvania - **Friends Life Care in Blue Bell at http://friendslifecare.org/**;

Tennessee - **Alexian Brothers in Chattanooga at http://www.alexianbrothers.net/www/docs/108/retirement-care-plan-planning-program-chattanooga;**

Types of Contracts

Type A, also known as extensive lifecare contracts

These are lifecare agreements that nominally offer a resident the most security. Nothing is free however. The entrance fees for Type A will be the highest, and all the contracts will provide that the monthly fees may be increased at certain periods (such as annually with 30 days' written notice).

The benefit is that typically the contract guarantees that you will pay the same rate regardless of your level of care. Keep in mind that as a USA average, assisted living fees are often twice as much as independent living's.

For you, there's never a difference. Residents in independent living, assisted living and skilled nursing all pay the same monthly rate.

These contracts provide housing, services and amenities including unlimited use of healthcare services.

The CCRC absorbs the risk that more residents than projected will need higher levels of care even if only temporarily, such as rehabilitation.

The US Department of Health and Human Services estimated that someone turning 65 today has a 70% chance of needing some type of long-term care.

The monthly fee you pay today in independent living may seem high to you but if you end up in skilled nursing facility eight years from today, it may turn out to be a bargain.

The financial risk for the resident is that the monthly fee may eventually exceed your monthly income. The contract should have language that indicates a 'benevolence' or similar fund will make up the difference.

If you are risk averse and value predictable costs, Type A is made for you. Additionally, you may be eligible to deduct from your income taxes a certain amount of prepaid health care built in your fee. The CCRC should provide that amount around tax time.

The CCRC usually requires a medical exam and a review of your financial profile before accepting you as a resident.

Type B, also known as modified lifecare contracts

These contracts offer lower entrance fees but limit the amount of health care services that may be accessed without any increase in the monthly fee.

For example, some may offer a limited stay, such as 120 days in a year in the skilled nursing facility for rehabilitation or after-surgery care, with no increase in the monthly fee. Others may not offer any health services.

If the resident requires care beyond that period, the resident usually pays market rates.

It is important to determine if the contract gives you any rights to assisted living, skilled nursing or memory care. The contract may give you priority access to this healthcare but not a guaranteed access as a Type A contract would.

Expect to have a medical review before the CCRC will accept you.

Type C, also known as 'fee for service' contracts

These contracts include similar housing, services and amenities as Type A and B contracts but require residents to pay market rates for any health-related services or nursing care under an as needed arrangement and for residence in assisted living, memory care or skilled nursing.

Type C contracts offer lower entrance fees, but the risk of large long-term care expenses remains solely with you rather than the facility.

Be sure to verify if the contract states you will receive priority placement if you want to transfer to a higher level of care.

Type D, also known as rental agreements

CCRC contracts also may be annual or pure month-to-month rentals, and all services beyond housing are either at market or pre-determined rates.

Some communities are open to federal or state-funded programs for low-income seniors. Inquire, if this is important to you one way or the other.

Type D is like renting an apartment. You may be required to pay a security deposit and first and last month's rent before moving into the community.

Meals and services normally come with additional charges, and all health care is paid by the resident at prevailing market rates.

A subset of Type D are standalone agreements for seniors who want to enter assisted living or a skilled nursing facility directly without starting in independent living. CCRCs allow this when they have vacancies in those higher-care facilities, and you pay current market rates.

The good news is that there are no entrance fees; you are not financially tied to the community and you can move if you're dissatisfied with the services.

The bad news is rentals do not guarantee lifetime care.

Because you haven't paid a substantial entrance fee, however, you can change communities if new management runs your facility into the ground or if you want a different level of care at a different facility.

Some communities have excellent independent living but limited or mediocre assisted living, or vice versa.

It's nice to be able to move to a community that better suits your needs without the burden of losing all or most of a large entry fee.

Do ask about the availability of additional services as you age or suffer a health setback.

Some communities offer a la carte services so you could stay in your rental even if you need help with meals, showering, getting dressed and groomed or other daily activities. Some communities are more rigid and might require you to move to assisted living.

Would you have any priority in rehabilitation services at the community? Many, many seniors suffer falls or surgeries that require some rehabilitation. Will you be able to get it onsite and still maintain your apartment?

A rental unit may make sense financially, but do consider your future.

Do you have family to help you in the event you need or want to move or suffer major health issues or are you so independent you don't have a support system?

Does the rental community have a social worker who could/would help you?

If you're a single without support, a rental might be fine for some period, but you may want to secure more support in a different type of contract once you reach your 80s or experience some worsening health issues.

Original Life Care

The CCRC concept was developed more than a century ago by religious and fraternal organizations that told their elderly members, "If you'll give me all your assets, I'll take care of you for life."

I don't think you'll find anyone still living who moved into a CCRC under these conditions, but there are still people around who think that's what a CCRC is and that you have to give them all your money when you enter. You don't (but the entrance fee may feel like they're getting most of your money).

Equity and Other Contracts

There are a handful of CCRCs organized as condominiums or cooperatives so that a resident is an equity holder or owner in the community or unit.

The difference between a condominium and cooperative is that in the former you own a specific unit and can sell it when you want whereas in a cooperative you are a stockholder and have a responsibility for the entire community. If you want to sell your share in the cooperative; i.e., your apartment, it requires the approval of the board of directors.

Some Equity CCRCs don't allow the resident to sell the unit in either case. The community sells it and then gives the proceeds minus selling costs including marketing, repairs, cleaning, painting, agent fees, closing costs and required community fee (if any) to the former resident or their estate.

A major concern is what happens if you need to move to another level of care. Do you sell your unit or does it revert to the community in return for some degree of healthcare coverage? These types of CCRCs, however, may be ideal for those with a good Long Term Care insurance plan.

The idea of being an equity holder in the CCRC may sound secure to you, but there are drawbacks. A synonym for equity often is liability.

Make sure you understand the financial and legal liabilities associated with your ownership position as these vary by state laws.

- What is your liability for lawsuits against the cooperative?
- What is your liability for mortgage or other loan payments?

- Could a bank place a lien on your personal property if the CCRC gets into financial trouble?
- Are you allowed to deduct any share of the mortgage/bond interest payments on your income tax?
- If you die, are your inheritors responsible to sell the unit? Will they have to keep making monthly payments until it's sold?

It is much easier to sell a condominium than a cooperative. The condo sale is like any home sale. You will be limited to senior buyers but otherwise have latitude in selling it.

In a cooperative, the board of directors must approve the buyer first. Occasionally, you'll read about a celebrity rejected by a cooperative board because they don't want all the publicity that comes with a celebrity.

With either a condo or coop, it will take time to sell the unit. That could tie up any inheritance for some time depending on how readily those types of units are selling.

Will you have a vote on what the CCRC is doing? Are there elections for the board of directors and could you serve as an officer?

Get the answers to these questions from your lawyer before you have a problem.

If you are serious about an equity CCRC, I really encourage you to have a local lawyer review the contract before you sign.

Your lawyer can advise you on what your state law and contract allow your equity CCRC to do, such as buying new properties, increasing fees, selling assets or entering contracts for other services.

Miscellaneous – senior communities

There is one other model that you should understand. Until recently, the largest nonprofit senior provider in the United States was **Evangelical Lutheran Good Samaritan Society at http://www.good-sam.com/** headquartered in South Dakota with residences in 22 states.

I write *until recently* because Good Sam is retrenching and is becoming a regional rather than a national provider with communities in only 7 states instead of the 15 states as of 2023. The organization is selling off its communities in the other 8 states.

While Good Samaritan locations usually offer all three levels of life care, it is not a CCRC in the sense that you have a guarantee of life care.

Good Samaritan was developed as a rental community with residents paying monthly fees that change/increase as the resident's level of care grows. The contract you signed was a standard rental agreement.

Many locations now offer an alternate plan where a resident in independent living pays an entry fee for a deeply discounted monthly fee.

The entry fee is refundable at some percentage, typically 70% to 90%, when the resident moves out for any reason, including moving to assisted living or SNF, regardless of how long the resident has been in independent living.

This is a more generous arrangement than many CCRCs today especially those that require your old unit to be occupied before you receive your refund.

Although you don't have a contractual guarantee of service if your money runs out, one of the ways these groups maintain nonprofit status with the Internal Revenue Service (IRS) is to pay for indigent residents.

I have never heard of any Good Samaritan resident forced out of a community for non-payment.

Bottomline

With more than 2,000 CCRCs nationwide, you should be able to find whichever type of business arrangement you want.

Six Key Item to Understand in the Contract

Be sure to get a copy of the CCRC's contract before you decide. Read it and consider having an attorney review it before you sign.

Since the CCRC drafted it, it's going to have provisions to protect the community. That's not necessarily bad, but you do need to understand a few things that you can expect to find in every contract.

1. You may be moved to another level of care at the community's discretion.

Almost all CCRCs will try to work with the resident and the resident's family, but community management will have the last word about whether a resident is forced into a different level of care.

If a resident requires too much attention in the dining room or needs home health services for more than a few weeks, many CCRCs will require that resident to move to assisted living.

Assisted living residents are often required to move when mental deterioration necessitates a placement in a locked memory care unit or 24/7 care is otherwise required.

Although the contract may have a provision for appeal, the facility almost always has the right to make the final decision.

2. You may be evicted.

If you selected a CCRC that doesn't accept Medicaid in its nursing facility and you run out of money, you may be moved to another (likely inferior) facility if you don't have a Type A contract. Yes, it does happen.

Even if you're healthy and living independently, you may be evicted with written notice if you cause too many problems for the other residents or persistently violate the rules of the community.

This is especially a problem in nursing facilities when some older people become extremely demanding or violent, or have difficult family members. Every community has some elderly people who've been moved from one facility to the next.

3. Your monthly fee will be increased.

Most contracts provide for annual fee 'adjustments' (which are always increases) with 30 or 60 days' written notice.

That is one reason why the CCRCs that guarantee you'll only pay one rate regardless of whether you're in independent living, assisted living or a nursing facility are not as fantastic a deal as they would lead you to believe.

That rate may become a real burden as you age if you're still living independently. You're helping subsidize the rate for the less healthy population even though you may not feel you're getting your share of the fee.

4. 'Life care' can be voided if you spend foolishly … or the CCRC does!

If you think you can give your savings to the Red Cross or your grandchildren because the CCRC is going to take care of you—think again. Most CCRC contracts provide that they are not responsible for your life care if you have deliberately or foolishly depleted your assets.

Look for language that states "after proper management and expenditure of resident's assets" if you run out of the money the CCRC will continue to provide care for you "as long as the resources of the CCRC are adequate for such purposes."

In addition, expect to be required to have Medicare Part A and Part B insurance or its equivalent. If you're in the SNF, you'll be required to apply for Medicaid when you can no longer pay yourself.

If the CCRC's 'benevolence' fund (or whatever they call it) runs out of funds, the CCRC could evict you. That's been a rare circumstance in the past decade, but it has happened.

5. Having a religious denomination's name doesn't mean the denomination is responsible for the CCRC.

Expect to see a paragraph that states something such as: "*Denomination X in whole or in part neither has nor accepts any responsibility for the financial or agreement obligations of this CCRC.*"

In other words, perform your due diligence and don't rely on a religious name to mean anything.

6. You may be temporarily placed in another facility.

You may be ready to move into the assisted living or nursing facility, but the CCRC may not have a vacancy.

The contract should provide that while the CCRC may place you in another comparable facility, you will be moved back to the CCRC's facility upon the next vacancy.

Any difference in cost between your CCRC and the temporary facility should be the responsibility of your CCRC.

Moving costs also should be the responsibility of the CCRC.

Bottomline

CCRCs often market aging-in-place, but you're not protected against future declines in quality of care or the cost of the care. Buyer beware (hence this book).

Entrance Fees

If the CCRC has an entrance fee, they usually will assess your financial situation before you both sign a contract.

Most CCRCs require you to have net assets of twice the amount of the entrance fee. This can be in liquid savings or investments such as 401(k) plans.

A few years ago, the standard practice was to offer refundable entrance fees or at least refund a significant portion, such as 90%, of the entrance fee. That's becoming less and less prevalent.

Refunds assumed a stream of new residents moving in and residents permanently leaving the CCRC based on actuarial tables. That was before people starting living longer.

According to the U.S. Bureau of the Census, in 1900 only one in every 25 Americans was considered elderly (85 or older). In 1990, about one in eight Americans was considered elderly. By 2020, the Census Bureau found that one in every six Americans was elderly.

With our weak economy, rising healthcare costs, reduced government health care reimbursements and longer-lived residents, many CCRCs have adjusted their refund policies.

Examine the CCRC's entrance fee policies carefully.

Do you pay more for a refundable fee?

Some CCRCs still offer refunds of a significant portion of the entry fee when a resident dies or leaves the CCRC, but only if the resident has paid an additional amount beyond the basic entrance fee.

For instance, a community may normally require a $200,000 entrance fee with no refund after 5 years.

If the resident pays an additional x-amount, y-percentage (example, $100,000 and 90%, respectively) of the entrance fee this will be refunded regardless of when and how the resident leaves the unit.

What is the timing of the refund?

Some CCRCs issue refunds only when the unit is reoccupied. This could involve quite a wait depending on the economy and other conditions; e.g., COVID requires a year-long shutdown.

Some CCRCs issue refunds after x-months or re-occupancy, whichever comes first.

See how the refund is prorated

The most frequent way I've seen refunds handled today is that a resident may receive x-percentage for each of the first four or five years of residency. After four or five years, there is no refund.

Make sure you understand what x-percent is and how it is calculated. Often a contract will provide for a monthly percentage rather than an annual one.

Almost all contracts provide for a non-refundable amount, such as 4%, for administrative or processing costs.

See if you have any protection

If you want some type of refund, the safest way to ensure it is to have a CCRC that puts some portion of the entrance fees into an escrow account.

Some states require that and provide a formula or specific amount that must be kept in a liquid account. This is no different than banks/credit unions that have x% of cash on hand rather than 100% of deposits in cash.

If there is no escrow account, you are considered an unsecured debtor and if the CCRC goes bankrupt, you may not have any of your refundable entrance fee returned to you.

See what happens if the resident dies

For single residents, contracts often provide for a percentage refund based on a sliding scale depending on how soon after moving in the resident dies.

For example, 50% of an entrance fee might be paid to the inheritors if the resident dies within the first two years of residency. After two years, there may be no refund.

For couples, contracts usually grant no right to refund of any portion of the entrance fee when just one member dies.

See if different levels of entrance fee are offered

Some CCRCs now offer 'capital preservation' or such nomenclature so that a resident pays a reduced entrance fee but has no rights to a refund.

This is an excellent alternative for someone who is not concerned about leaving an inheritance.

Others offer entrance fee amounts on a sliding scale depending on how great a percentage the resident wants returned.

These can be based on a limited number of years or forever. Obviously, the higher the refund percentage, the higher the entrance fee you will pay.

See what happens if you move to a new level of care

If you move from independent to assisted living or nursing care or back to independent living, is there a new entrance fee? I would hope not. If the CCRC provides refunds, are you qualified for a refund if your move to nursing care is assumed to be forever?

Think about the utility of refunds

The important question is not whether a CCRC offers a refund but whether it should.

Offering a refund during the first few years of occupancy is sensible as that gives residents time to see if the CCRC is a good fit for them and preserves a significant portion of their capital to be used to buy into another CCRC or other living arrangements.

In the long term, a better use of entrance fees is to fund capital improvements that benefit existing residents and entice new residents.

The typical CCRC uses the entrance fees to pay interest on bonds or other loans to update or expand the community

There have been lawsuits when some residents find out that entrance fees are not sitting a savings account or CD and readily available for refund upon request.

You can decide for yourself if it makes sense to have a large escrow account or if these are money-grubbing lawsuits.

If people aren't moving into independent living, the CCRC is unlikely to be able to continue operation for a long time, let alone refund an entrance fee.

Look at the long-term picture of how you want to live your golden years. CCRC residency should not be treated as an investment. It's about how you want to live now, not how you can leave a nice estate.

If you reared your children correctly, they are going to want you to have the best care you can for the rest of your life and won't worry about what they might or might not inherit.

If your children or grandchildren are greedy and offering lots of unsolicited advice about fees and how to protect your assets, ignore them or tell them to get a job.

Bottonline

When you're 90, it's too late to try to make up for 20 years of neglectful parenting by leaving your children an inheritance.

Six Ways to Fund the Entrance Fee (and Two Ways that Won't)

CCRCs typically want your assets to be at least two times the entrance fee value. How wonderful to have the liquid savings or proceeds to pay the entrance fee.

Many of us, however, are not that fortunate and look to the following for funding.

You sell your home

The housing market can make it difficult or easy for homeowner seniors to cover entrance fees. So much depends on your location, mortgage rates and the general economy.

Up to $250,000 profit (twice that for married couples) on the sale of a home is untaxed. Home sales traditionally have been the key way people pay CCRC entrance fees.

Your family helps out

Several CCRC managers have told me that this is becoming more common.

A couple or individual's children will step up and provide the entrance fee. Good for them.

[Children - be sure to read the chapter on *Filial Support*.]

You have long-term health insurance

This will not cover independent living or the entrance fee, but most long-term insurance policies issued since 2000 cover some of the monthly expenses for assisted living as well as nursing facility care.

Not all CCRCs, however, accept private insurance. If you're paying the entrance fee for independent living at a life care CCRC, this type of insurance is unnecessary.

You're a low-income veteran or surviving spouse and turn to the VA for help

If you're a veteran, the first place you should look for a CCRC is the communities, such as restricted to or marketed to military veterans.

If those are not where you want to live or otherwise not available to you, you may qualify for financial assistance from the Veterans Administration (VA).

Contact your local VA office and they will assign a care advisor to help you navigate the CCRC options and determine how much financial assistance you may receive.

The VA also helps with assisted living costs.

You take money from your retirement accounts

If the account is a Roth Individual Retirement Account (IRA), you're in luck. That money has already been taxed, so you won't have any penalties or owe any money to the IRS for using it.

If you have a 401(k), 403(b), or non-Roth IRA, the money you take from that account will be taxed as ordinary income. Plan accordingly when you withdraw the money; you may need to withdraw in excess of the entrance fee to pay your taxes.

I have more bad news. Since your Medicare Part B premium is based on your income tax return, the IRA distribution may raise your income above the normal premium level and cause Medicare to ask for a higher premium from you.

If this happens, do file an appeal and try to get the premium reduced on the basis of a onetime life-changing event.

You try a non-traditional approach

Sometimes people have a term life insurance policy that they sell to a third party for x-percentage of the face value and use that money for the fee.

This is called a viatical settlement and states have differing laws on how it is applied. One potential benefit to doing this is that proceeds of a life insurance policy are usually free from federal income tax.

A similar situation exists when someone is entitled to an inheritance or lawsuit settlement and sells their entitlement to the third party.

If you want to go this route, you should talk to an accountant and/or lawyer before signing with one of the companies that offer these services.

Laws also vary widely state to state on how these settlements are taxed.

Two that's won't work

You will rely on Medicare

Medicare does not pay for independent living even when you're over 65.

It doesn't pay for assisted living either (with very few strict exceptions) or the support needed for 'activities of daily living,' such as help to dress, bathe or use the bathroom.

Medical expenses such as rehabilitation or physical therapy that usually qualify under Medicare are covered but not daily living expenses.

Medicare will cover the costs of a limited number of days of rehabilitation in a nursing care facility, but make sure your doctor follows all the rules on how to admit you. You must go directly from a hospital to the rehabilitation/nursing home.

Medicare has and does deny claims because some arcane requirement was overlooked.

You will rely on Medicaid

Medicaid, for low-income seniors or when you've exhausted your other income, will pay for the SNF but rarely for assisted living. Do keep in mind that what is covered varies from state to state and sometimes even from county to county.

Some states participate in a program called Program of All-Inclusive Care for the Elderly (PACE) that may help with the costs of assisted living. Your state senior services agency or local senior center can help you find the right contact for more information. (See Resources chapter.)

It's worth reviewing your state's coverage before you decide on a CCRC location, but it's not foolproof since laws change and many states have drastically reduced coverage over the last few years.

Bottomline

It takes money to move into a CCRC – no way around that.

Monthly and Other Fees - Independent Living

Ideally you should have a monthly income at least two to two-and-a-half times the monthly fee you're being charged. In addition, there may be taxes assessed as explained below.

Basic monthly fee

Certainly, it should cover 'rent' of your unit, community maintenance, use of community facilities, planned transportation and whatever wellness activities and facilities the CCRC offers.

The following are some of the additional services that may or may not be included within the monthly fee: meals; housekeeping; unscheduled transportation; medical or nursing care provided in resident's unit; prescriptions; and individual personal care such as help with dressing, in the resident's unit.

Many CCRCs provide only a limited number of meals (say, one a week) in the basic monthly independent living fee but offer monthly discounts if you purchase x-number of meals.

Many facilities offer additional services, such as house cleaning or laundry, at defined prices.

Others do not and you may need or want to use local or franchised companies such as Merry Maids or Home Instead, etc.

Taxes

The most frequent 'other fee' you will be asked to pay is a tax that will be prorated by number of residents or by some combination of number of residents and the square footage of individual living units.

This is called an ad valorem tax assessment. The CCRC pays it and then prorates it among residents.

You pay it in addition to any other annual or monthly fees. The ad valorem tax pays for the CCRC's share of fire protection, police, roads and other services.

You may love the perceived security that comes from living in a gated community, but remember, all the roads and maintenance are then the responsibility of the gated community, not the city or county.

These gated or planned communities are sometimes part of a Community Development District (CDD), Municipal Utility District (MUD) or Planned Unit Development (PUD).

Ad valorem taxes or assessments can be expected to increase each year.

Get an estimate of what you will owe and what the increases have been over the past five years.

Bottomline

Make sure you understand what additional charges you'll be expected to pay in addition to the monthly fee.

Also ask for a list of the additional services, such as housecleaning, that the CCRC offers with their costs.

Monthly and Other Fees - Assisted Living (AL), Skilled Nursing Facility (SNF), Memory Care

Please read the preceding chapter on taxes and fees for independent living. The ad valorem tax is assessed in these living units as well.

Be cautious and obtain a written monthly estimate of the costs. There are no facilities that have more added-on costs than ALs and SNFs.

Assisted living monthly fee may not cover much

The basic assisted living fee may not cover more than 'rent,' some meals, an emergency call pendant or pull cord and access to the scheduled transportation and activities of the CCRC.

For example, some common additional fees include personal laundry (bedding and towels are usually included in the basic fee), help with showers, haircuts, telephone and help with medications. Cable TV may be included but Internet service usually is not.

If the resident needs help to organize medications by daily doses or to give insulin shots, there may or may not be an extra charge for this. I know one AL that charges $15 every time a nurse gives a resident a pill.

Don't assume that meals will be part of the basic package. Make sure you understand what, if any, meals are included and the cost of additional meals if the answer is none or only one a day.

Regularly scheduled transportation offered by the CCRC to all residents (independent and assisted) may be 'free.' If you need individual transportation to visit a doctor, there may be an additional fee.

Also understand what happens if the resident needs to go a hospital or to rehabilitation for some period of time. Will s/he continue to be charged for the AL room as well as the CCRC's SNF?

Getting additional help

ALs are intended to provide independence for their residents with additional security and access to expanded care.

Some CCRCs essentially allow independent living units to become ALs by letting the resident hire the additional help s/he needs to continue living there. This is great for those who want to stay in their independent living unit and can afford to pay for home health care.

At some point, it is going to be more expensive to keep paying for people coming in to help you than it would be to move to assisted living or a SNF.

Understand what the rules are at your CCRC and if there are any limitations on this or if the CCRC leaves it to the resident to determine when it makes financial sense to move into AL.

Some ALs use their own personnel to provide these services and some contract with home-help agencies such as Home Instead or Comfort Keepers. See if the contract allows you to hire your own helpers or if you must use the services of the CCRC.

SNFs and Memory Care

These costs require the same type of scrutiny although Medicare and Medicaid rules are rigid and provide more protection for residents than ALs which are state, not federally, regulated.

One important point about SNFs is that Medicaid will not pay for private rooms. At most CCRCs, residents privately pay for SNF care until their money runs out. Then the CCRC requires the resident to go on Medicaid.

If the resident wants a private room, however, the family may cover the additional cost without affecting the resident's Medicaid eligibility.

Bottomline

Do NOT assume anything about these facilities. Get in writing exactly what is included in the monthly fee and understand what additional services you may need to fund. Ask for a list of the additional services offered with their costs.

Resident Qualifications

While you're looking at potential CCRCs, the community also will be looking at you to see if you're a good candidate for residency. Here's what they're examining.

Age

By federal law, a resident must be 62 years or older to permit age discrimination in housing. The CCRC may allow couples if at least one is over 62.

Background

Many CCRCs now require all prospective residents to have a credit check. The CCRC must have your authorization to run your credit report and most will charge you a non-refundable fee to cover their cost for the report. This is separate from showing your net worth.

Texas requires assisted living and residential care facilities to screen residents as well as employees and include a check for sexual predators. Other states may have additional requirements.

Retirement communities can be havens for identity theft, fraud and property theft. Periodically, there are arrests from prostitution to drug dealing taking place in retirement communities.

In 2014, a California CCRC had a resident arrested for operating a methamphetamine lab in his retirement apartment. The resident was already on parole after a previous conviction for selling meth.

The news media tends to treat senior arrests as jokes ('over-the-hill-gang') but it's not funny when the neighbors of the criminals are vulnerable and easily coerced out of money or property.

In my opinion, background screening should be mandatory at every CCRC. Good communities require this for all residents and staff and the best ones also check sex offender and criminal registries.

If the CCRC doesn't care enough, or is too afraid of losing a potential resident to protect residents from meth dealers and sexual predators, don't move in there!

Financial qualifications

CCRCs usually want a resident to have a net worth twice the amount of the entrance fee and monthly income twice to two-and-a-half times the monthly fee.

There's usually some flexibility. For instance, if you don't meet the net worth requirement but you have a secure government pension that exceeds the monthly fee requirements, you may be accepted.

Copies of bank accounts, investment accounts, pensions, 401(k) or 403(b) accounts are usually sufficient.

Health

CCRCs will want either a doctor's statement that you are able to live independently and/or an examination by a staff member before you move in. Most CCRCs want this exam done within 30 or 60 days of your moving date.

Insurance

You will be required to have Medicare Part A and B insurance or equivalent. Many CCRCs also require a supplemental health insurance policy or equivalent. The CCRC won't take your word for it. They'll want a copy of your insurance cards.

Bottomline

A CCRC that doesn't verify health and financial status of new residents may be starting down the Highway of Financial Instability.

Who Lives in a CCRC?

Thanks to US News we have some information on residents of a CCRC or Life Plan community.

Age - Average age of a CCRC resident is 80 to 83. If the CCRC is older than ten years, the average age is 85 to 87.

Amenities - In order, the amenities potential residents look for in a CCRC are a fitness center, walking or bicycle path, library, bank and convenience store. For the individual units, it depends on emergency call systems, WIFI connectivity, patios or balconies and garages or covered parking.

Bedrooms - Almost 70 percent of the respondents were looking for a two-bedroom duplex or apartment.

Education - A majority of new residents are likely to have a college degree. In fact, CCRC residents are roughly twice as likely as the general over 65 population to have college degrees.

Entrance fees - Nearly 75 percent of CCRCs require an entrance fee and the majority still offer some type of refund. The average entrance fee was $400,000 with some CCRCs charging as much as $2-million.

Future - The Census Bureau reports that nearly 10,000 baby boomers turn 65 each day. By 2034, all of the baby boomers will be over 70. By 2030, seniors will comprise 20 percent of the total population. There are plenty of potential residents to fill the existing CCRCs.

Gender - Two-thirds of the new residents were women, although the number of men moving into CCRCs increased as the men aged. Every CCRC you tour, however, is going to have more female residents than male.

Importance - Prospective residents said they care about these five items: 1) financial transparency; 2) resident representation on board of directors; 3) social accountability (volunteer work in community); 4) access to transportation and 5) endowment for residents who have exhausted their financial resources.

Income – The average annual income of new residents is $66,000. About half of new and existing residents have a net worth close to $1M.

Location - The top ten states, in order, for number of CCRCs are Pennsylvania, Ohio, California, Illinois, Florida, Texas, Kansas, Indiana, Iowa and North Carolina.

Marketing - Referrals from existing residents account for more than 60 percent of all new resident move-ins. It's not uncommon to visit a CCRC and find two generations of families living there.

Marital status - Slightly more than half were widowed and about one-third were married couples.

Monthly fee – Average fee was $3,555 with increases of 2-5 percent a year in dependent living.

Ownership - About 80 percent of CCRCs are nonprofit. At least half are affiliated or the offspring of faith-based groups: 21 percent are Lutheran; 18 percent are Methodist; 14 percent are Presbyterian; and 12 percent are Catholic. (Keep in mind that the denomination is rarely financially liable for the CCRC.)

Planners - The term CCRC marketing employees use to describe the spouse or single person who evaluates the risks of potential long-term care and the elements of each CCRC community. These people take the initiative to find the right choice for care before it becomes critical. They drag the reluctant spouse along when they move in.

Reason for moving into a CCRC - A majority chose CCRCs because of concerns about increasing health care needs.

Residents – Average resident lives 10-12 years in independent living and 1-2 years in assisted living or SNF.

Satisfaction - 79% were very satisfied with their communities, 88% would do the move again and 88% would recommend their CCRC to a friend. Only two percent were very dissatisfied with their CCRC.

Sites - About 60% of CCRCs are part of multi-site systems while 39% are single-site CCRCs.

Size – Average CCRC is about 330 unites comprised of 231 independent living, 34 assisted living and 70 skilled nursing home beds. (I expect this to change dramatically over the next few years as discussed in Storm Clouds chapter.)

Turnoffs - The biggest turnoff for prospective residents is poor facility and ground maintenance. CCRCs that defer maintenance in an attempt to cut costs are being penny-wise.

Prospective residents emphasized the importance of maintained grounds and buildings while poorly kept facilities made them question whether the CCRC had the financial strength to meet future resident needs.

Eight Things You Should Look for in Any CCRC

1. Limit your choices to nonprofits.

One of the ugly things happening in senior care is the number of private equity companies buying nursing homes and CCRCs.

That doesn't mean for-profit places can't be wonderful. They can be—and, in fact, some of the plushest and most active CCRCs are for-profit. The for-profit facility may take even better care of residents than a money-strapped nonprofit.

The key difference is that, at the end of the day, the for-profit facility must have some profits to distribute to stockholders. Nonprofits can invest all monies in the operation and development of the CCRC.

If cash flow becomes a problem, the first thing for-profits will cut is staffing. If you're Warren Buffett, this is not a problem. If the CCRC starts to go downhill in services and reduces staffing to increase profits, you can move to another one.

If you're Warren Smith and you've invested most of your life savings in the entrance fee, moving to another CCRC may not be an option.

It is also more difficult to find a for-profit CCRC that will guarantee care for life. Nonprofit facilities, however, often have 'benevolence' funds that will kick in if your savings and pensions become inadequate to care for you.

The sad thing is that even starting with a nonprofit doesn't guarantee that it will always be that way. Some nonprofits have run into funding problems and sold out, often to these private equity groups.

The only thing you can do is try to make the best initial choice you can.

2. Decide if you want single site or multi-site facility.

Some CCRCs are part of a chain. For instance, ACTS Retirement-Life Communities has 21 communities in eight states.

Single site communities mean just that—they have no affiliation or connection with any other CCRCs.

Multi-site facilities can help each other and share resources and services as well as personnel and best practices.

Some allow a resident to transfer among communities. For example, if you started out in an independent living residence in Orlando but now want to move to the assisted living facility in Houston to be near your only child, you'll have a priority placement and not have to re-qualify. (Of course, you'll pay the Houston AL fees.)

Some residents don't like multi-site facilities because they feel the money they pay in entrance and monthly fees may be shared with facilities having financial struggles. The residents don't feel they're getting the benefit of all their payments.

The problem with single site communities is just that—your site stands or falls on its own and you're very much at the mercy of the competence of the executive director and the financial reserves of that one site.

There's no one right answer to this but you should be aware of the implications of both types of communities as you make your choice.

3. See how they treat their staff.

I'm amazed at how many articles and books I read on selecting a CCRC that never mentioned this.

You can get used to the Mediterranean architecture and Formica kitchen counters if the CCRC staff treats you with kindness and respect. You will never be happy in your Buckingham Palace replica if there is insufficient staff or surly staff members who spend all their time on their smartphones.

You want a CCRC that values their employees and rewards them. Look around for pictures and parking spaces for the 'Employee of the Month'.

As you take facility tours, ask about staff turnover. Ask the CCRC if they offer training and advancement opportunities for their employees.

Ask them if they allow tipping. The answer should be '*No*', which reinforces the idea that staff members are expected to treat all residents equally. It is, of course, permissible if residents do take up a collection at Christmas and treat all the staff to a monetary gift.

As you meet staff members, whether it is the maintenance manager or the executive director, ask them how long they've worked there.

If the CCRC treats its employees poorly and only pays minimum wage, how well do you think those employees are going to treat the residents?

At the same time, the CCRC should value its residents enough to insist on credit checks and criminal background checks for all employees. Ask the prospective residence what they do.

4. Look for onsite physical and speech therapy.

We all dread the worst-case scenario of ending up in a nursing home.

The happy reality, from the U.S. Census Bureau, is that only about 25 percent of seniors live permanently in SNFs.

What is more likely to happen is that you will have an accident or take a fall.

Many people break ankles, feet and arms. People develop neck problems or strain their backs. Worse, they have strokes or heart attacks.

You want a facility that offers physical and speech therapy.

The alternative is that you have to drive or obtain transportation three or more times a week for 4-6 weeks for treatment.

How much nicer to have this capability within the CCRC and only have to walk over to the Wellness building that houses a physical therapy suite.

5. Ensure there are adequate medical facilities nearby.

Consider the proximity of any CCRC to medical facilities, especially those highly rated for treatment of heart disease and cancer (two looming problems for seniors). How nice to be within short driving distances of the Cleveland Clinic or Mayo Clinic.

If your facility is in a small town, are there doctors in town who still take new Medicare patients? Call any local clinics and say you're a new resident on Medicare. Is there a primary care doctor accepting new Medicare patients?

What about Medicare assignments (i.e., the doctor accepts the Medicare fee schedule as payment in full. If not, the doctor may charge 15% more than the Medicare fee schedule.)?

It's a plus if the city where the CCRC is located has a medical school or medical school patient care facility.

I am not a fan of small-town medicine, but if you insist on small-town living, at least make sure you can get to a regional or large facility for long-term treatment. If there's only one hospital within a reasonable distance, you are taking a risk.

Does the CCRC have a physician or nurse on duty at certain hours? Can you call someone within the CCRC 24/7? Does the CCRC bring in visiting doctors or specialists? Don't wait until you or your spouse has a heart attack to find out these things.

6. Look for financial soundness and occupancy rate.

We'll cover financial soundness in detail in a later chapter. The key items for now are how much long-term debt does the community have and what is its occupancy rate?

For a new community, lenders typically want 90% occupancy; i.e., contracts signed by people wanting to move in as soon as the community is built. New or under construction facilities are a risk. You can get a beautiful place and have the ability to customize it for yourself, but you run the risk that the community may never reach a self-supporting state.

I would be worried if a community occupancy rate dropped below 85% and worried sick if the community still had significant long-term debt. A well-run, well-priced CCRC is likely to have a waiting list.

I would expect the entrance fees to be used for construction or other long-term debt and the monthly fees to be used for normal operating costs.

In general, CCRCs rely on newer, healthier residents to provide entrance fees that help support the ongoing costs of the assisted living and nursing facility.

One caution: age is not always a reliable predictor. Some communities run into trouble after a decade or more of successful operation because they no longer acquire enough younger residents providing entrance fees for independent living.

A community that can't meet the desires of baby boomer residents may soon find itself in a precarious position.

7. Verify the nursing facility accepts Medicaid and can treat dementia patients.

Most nonprofits accept Medicare and Medicaid in their nursing homes.

Many for-profit facilities exclude Medicaid. Those that do, however, may limit the number of beds that are assigned to Medicaid. Ask about the ratio of Medicaid to non-Medicaid beds.

If you exhaust your personal funds and the facility has no open Medicaid beds, you could be required to move unless you live in a state (very few do) that prohibits this practice.

You also want a facility that can treat you forever if you become incapacitated with something like Alzheimer's. Verify that there is a locked ward or area for dementia patients or memory care support.

8. Rule out living units with gas appliances.

Unfortunately, seniors over 65 are far more likely than the general population to die in kitchen fires.

I understand gas heat may be cheaper than electric. I understand that many over-85-year-olds are perfectly capable of turning on and off stove tops with gas flames and are able to smell gas leaks.

It will be just your luck, however, to live next door to an 88-year-old who doesn't remember how to turn on and off the gas stove top, is hard of hearing, has no sense of smell and doesn't remember how to use a pilot light.

All electric facilities also tend to be newer than those that still have gas heat.

Bottomline

Stack the deck in your favor before you move in. Too many things are going to be out of your control once you're there.

Convincing a Family Member(s) to Move

All over America there are adult children trying to convince aging family members to leave their now too large and too high-maintenance homes and move into a CCRC. Here are a few suggestions to help you achieve that goal.

Start early

Once parents or family members are nearing retirement age, it's time to start discussing long-term plans.

The worse situation is to wait until an aged relative is suffering from some form of dementia, which may appear as extreme stubbornness, and then try to convince them to move.

It's reasonable to discuss wills and power of attorneys with your parents or family members. Tell them what you've done for yourself. Ask them to make these decisions now while they are healthy. The family should understand one another's wishes.

Remind your parent(s) that if you have this medical power, you can grant a hospital permission to treat or operate on them if they're injured in a car accident or some other calamity and not able to speak for themselves.

If you have a medical power of attorney, you may be able to enlist the doctor's support in convincing your parent it's time to move. Older people often will pay more attention to their doctor than their children.

It's also a good idea to have a financial power of attorney so you can help control their finances as they age. This may be more threatening to a senior than the medical power of attorney so tread lightly.

Don't nag

No parent is going to appreciate having his/her children tell them they are so old and infirm that they need to move to an old folk's home. That's not the reality, of course, but that's what many seniors will hear. Losing their independence is a major, major fear of most people.

Ask them to go with you to tour a facility

If you're a baby boomer, tell your parents you're thinking about a CCRC for yourself in the future and want to explore some facilities now, especially since some have long waiting lists.

That should be the truth but it also should be a way to get your parents to see how nice CCRCs are today. They need to understand it's not a bunch of old people sitting around a nurse's station.

If your parents or other family members know someone who lives in a CCRC, all of you should go visit that person together. Make sure you tour the entire community and that they see all of the activities available to them.

Do discuss the consequences of one aging parent

One parent, especially the mother, may often be more willing to recognize the problems in caring for a declining spouse.

If one parent has serious and debilitating diseases, the other one is probably fearful about whether s/he will be able to continue to help that spouse.

Discuss the benefits of a CCRC and how they can get help while still being able to live together.

The benefit of having scheduled transportation and on-call emergency help may be significant selling points.

Gently point out that when one spouse passes, the other will have the continued support of the CCRC staff and the friendships from the other residents.

Point out the safety in living in a CCRC

If your family member has a close call, such as falling or tripping, but without serious injury, note that residents of CCRCs always have someone available to call for help.

CCRCs usually have guards patrolling at night and emergency call buttons in units.

Some CCRCs require residents to push a button by 10 a.m. each morning so the community knows they are safe and well. Stress the security that comes with that kind of concern.

Help them prepare a financial analysis

If your parents use a financial planner, suggest they review the costs of staying in their home versus moving into a CCRC.

If they don't, you might just show them a typical analysis (most CCRCs offer this type of thing as part of their marketing materials).

Sometimes, when people hear the monthly fee, they think they could never afford it when, in reality, they spend more taking care of their home.

This is especially true if elderly owners are now paying people to do lawn care, cleaning and other maintenance.

Lay down the law

Some elderly people expect their children or other relatives to be on call 24/7 and otherwise provide them continual care so they don't have to go to the old folk's home. This situation is even worse when the senior has suffered mental deterioration.

You may have no choice but to tell them there's no alternative and take them to the AL or SNF. That sounds horribly cruel but, at some point, someone 90+ can no longer live alone.

Sometimes seniors who are forced into AL adjust well after three or so months and enjoy the social aspects of having friends their own age around.

If you're moving a senior relative into a SNF or memory care, don't expect a happy ending. They may be miserable.

You can ask the SNF about getting emotional support for them, even if it's just a few visits from the chaplain.

Enlist legal help

If you don't have medical or financial power of attorney (these are two separate powers), you should ask a local lawyer for help.

It's an arduous and unpleasant process to have an elderly family member declared incompetent and to have the court appoint a legal guardian.

You need to discuss this with an attorney and understand that courts typically expect an overwhelming degree of evidence before they will take away an elderly person's independence.

Warning to greedy relatives

We were sad when the wife of an 80-something couple passed away. We noticed that the couple's children did not visit as often as they did when the mother was still alive. After a year or two, they rarely even called their father.

Happily, he met a nice nurse's aide at the CCRC. She was 25 years younger and re-energized his life. When he told his children he was going to remarry, they hit the roof and accused the lady of being a gold digger.

The children got a lawyer to try to have their father declared incompetent so they could take control of his large estate. Guess what? The judge ruled in the father's favor.

The man married his girlfriend, moved into a larger new home in the community and cut his children out of his will. This was a happy ending in my opinion, but that isn't always the case.

Sometimes caregivers do take advantage of lonely seniors. You'd be surprised how often May/December romances and marriages happen at retirement communities. As I said, consider this a warning if you're hoping to inherit.

Bottomline

Be supportive but stress the need to plan ahead and the ability to make choices for themselves now while they are in good health. Many seniors hate to lose any independence, but they hate to be a burden even more.

Filial Support May Surprise Your Children

Most of us would like to be able to help our elderly parents when they need it, including helping them pay for assisted living or nursing care. In some states, that may be more of a requirement than a hope.

There's a history for it

Approximately 29 states have 'filial support' or 'filial responsibility' laws that date back from frontier days. These require a person's children to offer financial support to a parent.

Only nursing homes in Pennsylvania and South Dakota—so far—have sued relatives under these laws.

Children have been sued

In one widely publicized Pennsylvania case, a nursing home successfully sued a couple for $300,000 to cover the cost of their late father's care in a nursing home and ongoing care of the mother who had dementia.

The couple couldn't believe they were responsible for someone else's debts, even their parents', and contested the lawsuit. They lost but plan to appeal.

At least Pennsylvania law only makes children responsible if they can pay, and the couple in this case say they are living paycheck to paycheck.

Nursing homes are between a rock and a hard place

Profit margins at most nursing homes hover at just under 9 percent, according to a Medicare study almost 12,000 nursing homes.

Industry representatives have complained about meagre Medicaid reimbursements at the federal level and cash-strapped states are cutting back Medicaid funding even more.

A lawyer for the nursing homes said the lawsuits are sometimes used to force a family to apply for Medicaid so the home can receive some reimbursement.

At times, the family is asked to cover what Medicaid has not paid if there appear to be sufficient assets.

Bottomline

If your parent is going into an SNF, it's worthwhile to talk to a lawyer experienced in your state's elder laws regarding what you might be responsible for and how to obtain the required powers of attorney from your parent(s) so you can apply for Medicaid for them.

In any case, never sign papers making yourself responsible for your parent's financial expenses. The CCRC may ask you to do this but stress to them that your parent is the sole responsible person.

Six Special Concerns for Spouses

If you're moving with a spouse, you need to review the CCRC contract and community rules to understand the what-ifs involving spouses.

1. If you're not legally married, will the CCRC accord your partner the same rights as a spouse?

Some couples, heterosexual and homosexual, live together for years without legal matrimony. If that is your situation, you need to understand what your status is within the CCRC. Don't guess or assume what the law is. Ask the community management and review your contract.

2. What happens when one person moves to another level of care?

If you paid an entrance fee for independent living, you probably do not want to, or may be financially unable to, pay a new entrance fee for assisted living, skilled nursing facility or memory care. Ensure this is spelled out in the contract.

There's still the issue of a monthly fee. Will you now, probably, be paying two separate monthly fees? The person remaining in independent living should at least see a reduction.

Sadly, I see this over and over. One spouse is in SNF or a dementia ward while the other remains in independent living. This is an expensive way to live.

At my CCRC, spouses may live in AL units even if one resident is capable of independent living. The CCRC has also configured SNF rooms to allow couples to live together when both require nursing care.

3. What happens if you separate or divorce?

Will that impact any refund of the entrance fee? Could it be evenly split or determined by divorce decree?

If you both want to stay in the CCRC, would the spouse leaving the current residence have to pay a new entrance fee?

4. If you're in a CCRC that refunds some portion of the entrance fee, how does the death of one spouse impact that?

The answer may be that no refund is given until both residents are out of the CCRC or there may be a partial refund available at the time of one spouse's death. See what the contract says.

5. What if you get married while you are a CCRC resident?

Could you move to another level of care or another housing unit without paying a new fee? It's not unheard of for people to meet and marry while being residents of CCRCs and want to move to a larger apartment or house. What are the CCRC's rules for that?

6. Are there any special rules for dining and activities?

Some CCRCs attempt to segregate independent living, assisted living and nursing facility or memory care residents for dining.

That's often not the CCRC's idea but rather it is the preference of the residents who do not like seeing so many walkers and infirm people in the dining room. Maybe they don't like seeing what may lie ahead for them.

If you're in independent living and your spouse is in assisted living, will you be able to eat your meals together? Typically, any resident who goes to court to allow this wins their case.

As I noted, the problem more often is other independent living residents, not the CCRC management.

Are activities such as game nights or trips to museums available to all levels of residents or do assisted living and nursing facility residents have separate activities and trips? If the latter are separate, could you still go with them?

Bottomline

Don't assume. Ask and see what's in the contract. Even if something is not in the contract, you might request a written explanation of the regulations.

This is one area that can make living very unpleasant for spouses who still want to spend as much time together as possible.

Gay and Lesbian Retirees

Housing discrimination is illegal and some states explicitly protect the rights of gay and lesbian citizens.

Legal doesn't necessarily equate to welcoming, however, when it comes to retirement communities.

One lesbian couple really liked a CCRC they toured until they asked the marketing director whether they'd fit into the community. She advised them to tell people they were sisters.

Be upfront with the marketing people

As the couple above did, let the marketing person know that you are a gay or lesbian couple and ask about the reception you can expect.

Ask if there are other similar couples within the community.

The verbal and nonverbal responses you receive will provide a good indication of the community's attitudes.

Test before you buy

Go to the cafeteria or dining room for every meal. Introduce yourself and **your partner** to everyone you meet.

You'll quickly get a feel for the attitudes there.

Many CCRCs offer free or low-cost overnight stays for potential residents who tour the facilities.

Some communities also offer temporary rentals and some let you live there for 3 to 6 months before you have to sign a long-term contract and pay a rental fee.

Take advantage of those and test the waters.

Look for new communities

Many existing CCRCs started out as faith-based developments and many religions did or still do object to gay and lesbian couples.

Those beliefs may exist among older members of that faith—even though the community will comply with federal laws.

On the other hand, both existing and new residents of CCRCs nationwide are more likely to be college graduates.

Baby boomers moving into newer communities are even more likely to be well educated, sophisticated and products of corporate employers who supported diversity in the workplace.

New trends in communities

While communities may be more than happy to have this segment of seniors entering CCRCs, the existing residents may not be so welcoming.

As a result, we have CCRCs targeted to the lesbian, gay, bisexual, and transgender (LBGT) communities. See the following.

The first one to offer the full continuum of independent, assisted living and dementia care was Fountaingrove Lodge at **http://fountaingrovelodge.com/**in Santa Rosa, CA.

The John C. Anderson is an apartment building in Philadelphia at **https://www.pennrose.com/apartments/pennsylvania/john-c-**

anderson-apartments/ which caters to the low-income LGBT community. It opened in 2014 and has a 100-person waiting list.

Also serving the gay and lesbian community:

A Place for Us at **https://www.apfuhousing.com/** is 55+ rental community near Cleveland, OH catering to low-income LGBTQ seniors.

Birds of a Feather at **http://www.birdsofafeather.com/our-community/our-vision.html,** n Santa Fe, NM;

Carefree Cove at **https://www.dlasheville.com/carefree-cove-an-lgbtq-log-home-community-in-boone-nc/** with 165 acres of woodland in Zionville, NC

Living Out, an apartment community in Palm Springs, CA, at **https://livingout.com/**.

The Palms of Manasota at **https://palmsofmanasota.net/** in Palmetto, FL is located near Tampa Bay and offers 21 standalone homes.

Rainbow Vista at **https://www.rainbowvista.com/** in Gresham, OR is an apartment community for active seniors only with no assisted living or memory care.

The Resort at Carefree Boulevard is a lesbian only retirement community consisting of manufactured homes and recreational vehicles at **https://www.resortoncb.com/** in Fort Myers, FL.

Stonewall Gardens offers assisted living in Palm Springs, CA at **https://www.stonewallgardens.com/** in a small community in a very upscale city.

Triangle Square in Los Angeles, CA is a 62+ apartment community at **https://www.trianglesquareapts.com/**. This location provides many activities and recreation opportunities.

Village Hearth is a small 55+ community in Durham, NC at **https://www.villagehearthcohousing.com/** and a cohousing community with cottage style homes in a row with shared walls.

Bottomline

Laws are one thing; attitudes are another. Take your time and find a community that will accept you. They're out there.

Also read the chapter on *Six Special Concerns for Spouses*. Those apply to any couple.

Affinity Retirement communities - Alumni, Military, Religion, Other

It's easier than ever to find a retirement community supportive of what you want to do and the types of neighbors you want. Not all of the below are CCRCs, but they do offer retirement living.

Alumni and school-based

One of the newer trends is to have CCRCs near or associated with universities. For example, one upscale community called **Longhorn Village at http://www.longhornvillage.com/** is in vibrant Austin, TX, the home of the University of Texas.

This upscale CCRC was developed in association with the Ex-Students' Association of the University of Texas (UT) and offers a range of living units from apartments to custom-made homes with entrance fees starting in the five figures and going up to the seven figures.

Although Longhorn Village is open to anyone, think how happy UT alumni and rabid football fans are to live around their own kind!

Another operation is the Village at Penn State at **http://retireatpennstate.org/**, a nonprofit CCRC in State College, PA.

Other retirement communities associated with colleges include:

Florida - Oak Hammock at **http://www.oakhammock.org/** with the University of Florida in Gainesville;

Indiana – Holy Cross Village at **https://holycrossvillages.org** at Notre Dame in South Bend;

Massachusetts - **Lasell Village** at http://www.lasellvillage.com/with Lasell College in Newton;

New York - Longview **at https://longviewithaca.org** with Ithaca College in Ithaca; and

North Carolina - The Forest at **http://www.forestduke.org/** with Duke in Durham.

The Kendal Corporation at **http://www.kendal.org/** has developed several nonprofit CCRCs associated with or near colleges in the eastern part of the United States. Kendal states it offers "Communities and Services Enriching the Lives of Older Adults in the Quaker Tradition."

Quakers—or, more formally, the Religious Society of Friends—were a leader in developing senior communities and operate several high-quality, well-regarded communities.

If you like Ohio, Kendal_at **https://kao.kendal.org** in Oberlin is only mile from Oberlin College and near Cleveland.

It offers a wide variety of lifelong learning and almost 40 percent of its residents are former students or faculty.

For a list of current college-linked retirement communities, visit **https://www.universityretirementcommunities.com/**

Careers

Some communities are established for people who worked in certain fields or for certain unions.

Actorsfundhome.org in Englewood, N.J. provides rehabilitation, AL and SNF for entertainment professionals.

The National Association of Letter Carriers (an AFL/CIO union) sponsors a CCRC in central Florida called **Nalcrest** at **http://www.nalc.org/member-benefits/nalcrest**.

If you're a union member, you should be able to obtain information for their headquarters on retirement homes.

Military retirees

Some of the best run CCRCs are, deservedly so, reserved for combat veterans and retired military or their surviving spouses.

Some are restricted to retired officers while others have opened to federal civil service retirees or others.

Check out the locations that interest you and see how expansive the eligibility requirements are:

California - **Paradise Valley Estates** at **http://www.pvestates.com/** in Fairfield;

District of Columbia - Knollwood at Veteran Housing in Northern VA **https://www.armydistaff.org/about/**and the Armed Forces Retirement Home at **https://www.afrh.gov/washington**.

Florida - Air Force Enlisted Village at **http://www.afenlistedwidows.org/**for indigent surviving spouses in Shalimar;

Texas - two Air Force Villages at **http://www.blueskiesoftexas.org/** and one Army Retirement Community at **http://www.armyresidence.com/**, all in San Antonio;

Virginia - Falcons Landing at **https://www.falconslandng.org/about** Potomac Falls; Vinson Hall http://www.vinsonhall.org (Navy, Marine, Coast Guard) in McLean; and Patriots Colony at **http://www.riversideonline.com/patriotscolony/**in Williamsburg;

Washington - Patriot's Landing at **https://www.careage.com** in DuPont.

Religious affiliations

For example, if you're a Catholic, the Alexian Brothers have a life care community in Signal Mountain, TN at **https://www.ascensionliving.org/en/find-a-community/alexian-village-chattanooga-tn**, just 15 minutes from Chattanooga, while the Franciscan Sisters of Chicago operate Franciscan Village at **https://franciscanministries.org/franciscan-village/** in Lemont, IL just 27 miles from downtown Chicago.

Both facilities, and the others that both groups operate, welcome residents of any faith and all will be treated with respect.

The affiliation does mean a stronger Catholic orientation and values than you would find at more secularized CCRCs. (It does not mean they will be less expensive than other CCRCs; they won't.)

Sometimes the affiliation is even stronger. For example, Landow House at **http://www.hebrew-home.org/site/PageServer?pagename=landow_homepage** e in Rockville, MD appeals to Jewish seniors including Orthodox Jews.

There are three kosher meals a day, Friday evening Shabbat services and a Yiddish club.

Although not a formal CCRC, LutherHaven at **http://www.lutheranhaven.org/index.php** in Oviedo, FL has the three levels of life care but you must be a Lutheran and at least 65 years old to move into independent living.

The nonsectarian ElderSpirit Community at **http://www.elderspirit.net/** describes itself as "a community of mutual support and late life spirituality that has come to fruition in a mixed-income, co-housing neighborhood in Abingdon, VA."

Your church or religious community is a great place to get referrals.

RVs

If you've been a full-time RVer (recreational vehicle) and don't want to give up your RV, there's the nonprofit Escapees Care Center at **http://www.escapeescare.org/** in Livingston, TX. You live in your RV but receive three meals a day.

Others

ShantiNiketan at **https://www.facebook.com/shantiniketan.us/** is a 55+ condominium retirement community for people of Indian heritage. They have facilities or plans to build in Florida, California, Illinois, the District of Columbia and New Jersey.

Aegis Gardens at **http://www.aegisliving.com/aegis-living-of-aegis-gardens/** is an assisted living community for Asian-Americans in Fremont, CA. Feng Shui consultants helped design and decorate the facility. Staff members speak Mandarin and Cantonese and Tai Chi classes commence at sunrise each morning.

Enso Village at **https://www.kendal.org/community/enso-village/** is a CCRC devoted to Zen tradition in the wine country of Northern California. This was developed by the Kendal Corporation and proved so popular, Kendal is building another one in Southern California.

Nalanda Estates at **https://www.nalandaestates.com/** is a newly opened Indian retirement community in Florida on 30-acres with 83 homes.

Bottomline

No matter what your interests, there's likely to be a CCRC that appeals to you.

Taxes – The Good

NOTE: The following is designed to provide accurate information but it is not legal, accounting or professional advice. Seek assistance from an accountant, CPA or enrolled agent before you claim this deduction.

You may get a tax break

If you move into a CCRC that requires a non-refundable entrance fee and the contract includes healthcare, the Internal Revenue Service (IRS) views that as a pre-payment expense for healthcare services.

If entrance fees are fully or partially refundable, the deduction only applies to that portion of the fee which is not returned to the resident or their estate.

In addition to entrance fees, a portion of the monthly residential fees at CCRCs may also be tax deductible.

The logic underlying both deductions is that payments entitle residents to lifetime health care as part of their residential agreement, so a portion of their expenses really represents the cost of future healthcare benefits.

If you're in a Type D or rental arrangement, only the payments explicitly made for medical services would be tax deductible.

Your CCRC should provide you with an estimate of the deductions.

The deductible percentage varies by community depending on how they structure their expenses. As an example, ACTS Retirement-Life

Communities recently estimated that 36.18 percent of entrance fees and 38.61 percent of monthly fees are deductible as prepaid healthcare expenses.

This benefit arose thanks to a court decision.

This benefit is based on a 2004 Tax Court decision—Delbert L. and Margaret J. Baker v. Commissioner of the IRS.

The Bakers lived in a two-bedroom, two bath independent living duplex in an upscale community. They had an emergency pull cord system in their home and access to medical services from the CCRC's on-site health center. They could also take advantage of other wellness amenities such as a pool, spa and exercise facilities.

The Bakers claimed medical deductions equal to about 27 percent of their first year entry fee and about 40 percent of their monthly fees, but the IRS allowed only 19 percent of the monthly fees.

The Bakers decided to take their case to tax court and won. Their only losing argument was an attempt to claim medical deductions for CCRC expenses allocable to the community's swimming pool, spa and exercise facilities.

These types of expenses aren't deductible if taking advantage of them is simply beneficial to your overall health as opposed to treatment for a specific medical condition.

Bottomline

You're allowed to claim a deduction for prepaid medical expenses, regardless of the CCRC resident's current health status.

Since the fees we are talking about can be quite steep, significant deductions may be allowed despite the (current) 7.5 percent of adjusted gross income floor for deductible medical expenses.

Review that with a tax professional before you file for it!

Taxes – The Bad

Every state exempts some or all of the properties owned by charitable nonprofits from property taxes.

Cash-strapped cities and states, however, are beginning to question the validity of granting property tax and other exemptions to nonprofit CCRCs.

In many states, having federal IRS nonprofit status does not automatically mean the community is relieved of property taxes.

That's especially a concern when luxury CCRCs, such as those with bay or ocean views, require $1M or more in entrance fees and thousands of dollars in monthly fees from high-income residents.

It's especially concerning when some of these communities use tax-exempt bonds to finance construction.

Some cities are attempting to impose taxes or fees on nonprofits under the heading of PILOTs (payments in lieu of taxes) without regard for any legal right to do so.

States and Cities

Various states have made attempts to find a way to tax retirement community property.

Efforts have included trying to end nonprofit and religious exemptions for any property tax, trying to cap the sales tax refunds available to nonprofits and allowing cities to impose an 'essential services fee' on nonprofits.

So far, these have been unsuccessful but who knows the future.

Cities as varied as Anchorage, Boston and New Orleans have proposed ways to tax the property of nonprofits or to charge fees or payments for essential services such as fire and police.

National Council of Nonprofits statement

Charitable nonprofit organizations throughout the United States are dedicated to the public good; their work improves lives, strengthens communities and the economy, and lightens the burdens of government, taxpayers, and society as a whole.

Consistent tax policies at the federal, state, and local levels are critical to the success of charitable nonprofits in pioneering and implementing solutions to community problems and aspirations.

The National Council of Nonprofits is committed to preserving the tax-exempt status of organizations contributing to the well-being of their communities.

What this means for CCRC residents

If CCRCs do have to pay taxes or fees, expect the CCRC to apportion these costs to residents as part of the monthly fee.

If a resident can't absorb the added costs, the community's benevolence fund will be asked to pay.

This is not something any currently operating CCRC expected to fund and might have a detrimental effect on the community's benevolence fund for impoverished residents.

Bottomline

You're still a voter. Don't vote for these clowns who want to tax charities and use the money to buy votes from one group or the other.

Taxes – The Ugly

If the thought of paying property taxes isn't frightening enough, there is a worse calamity that could befall a CCRC—the IRS revokes the community's nonprofit status.

It's not an idle threat. Over the last 20 years, the IRS has revoked the tax-exempt status of more than 275,000 nonprofit groups because they failed to file required tax forms.

The consequences of this are that the CCRC becomes a for-profit (even if there are none) corporation and must pay taxes.

Those states or cities that do grant exemptions to nonprofits are now free to levy property and other taxes on the CCRC.

Even worse, losing tax exemption means the end of foundation and educational grants as well as a loss of donations and volunteer help.

This is truly a scary situation for any nonprofit CCRC and could even result in bankruptcy.

Ways to protect nonprofit status

Besides filing required forms in a timely manner, there are other checks that the IRS looks for in a true nonprofit. This is an oversimplification, but the key tests are below.

Suitable housing under the generic term 'homes for the aging'

The IRS expects the CCRC to provide residences that are designed to meet some combination of the physical, emotional, recreational, social, religious or similar needs of aged persons.

Examples of this would be fire-resistant construction materials, wide doorways and grab-bars, slip resistant flooring, 24-hour emergency alarm services and indoor/outdoor lounge areas.

Healthcare

The IRS doesn't require an on-site medical facility.

It's enough to have agreements with other facilities or healthcare personnel to serve residents.

CCRCs also are expected to provide transportation for medical examination and follow-up treatment and provide 24-hour emergency support.

Financial security

CCRCs must have a policy to continue care for residents who become impoverished.

This, however, doesn't prevent CCRCs from limiting initial admittance to those who are able to pay the fees.

Other steps the CCRC should take

The CCRC's incorporation papers, bylaws, mission statements and marketing materials should explain its charity policies and procedures.

Once a year expect to receive a form asking you to document how many hours you contributed in charity work and other volunteer services.

Meanwhile, the CCRC itself is documenting how many services, facilities and activities, especially free ones, it provided to the general public and to vulnerable populations.

It also will document shortfalls from federal and state government in reimbursement of services in assisted living and nursing homes.

Bottomline

One newer CCRC has beautiful single-family homes with views of the Gulf of Mexico. The entrance fees range from $800,000 to almost $2M with monthly fees for a single person ranging from $3,500 to $5,500 a month.

Many politicians are looking at such places and wondering why the CCRC is entitled to tax exempt status.

The battle is only beginning and those of us in much less grandiose communities can only hope we don't get caught in the crossfire.

Governance and Resident Rights

In theory, the executive director of the CCRC implements the policies of the Board of Directors.

If your CCRC is one of a multi-site group, that may be how it works. I know one chain that requires an individual site to obtain headquarters approval to spend more than $5,000 on any one purchase. That level of micromanagement may not please its employees, but it offers protection to residents.

If your CCRC is a single site facility, the likely scenario is that the director does whatever s/he wants because board members either don't understand what's going on or (mistakenly) think being a director is an honorary position and take at face value everything the director says.

(As I said in this book's description, this is a realistic guide.)

What the law requires

The IRS has guidelines for nonprofit boards and publishes the *Compliance Guide for 501(c)(3) Public Charities* at **http://www.irs.gov/pub/irs-pdf/p4221pc.pdf**.

The IRS can't require implementation, however, but has indicated that nonprofits that fail to adopt certain policies have a greater chance of being audited than those that do.

Directors do have a fiduciary responsibility and do have potential liability if they are negligent. In practice, I found no instances of board members being successfully sued except in cases of fraud or gross financial mismanagement (e.g., using CCRC funds to issue zero-interest loans to one another).

States may enact laws but don't count on strict enforcement. One story making the rounds of senior housing blogs described how a lawyer representing a group of dissident residents visited the state insurance office that regulated the CCRC.

The CCRC in question had dutifully filed the required annual paperwork. The state office showed the lawyer the file with the documents—all of them in unopened envelopes. The state office was short of staff so they simply filed the documents without any examination and without even opening the envelopes.

Resident rights

People who pay six, and sometimes seven, figure entrance fees to a CCRC are often unpleasantly surprised to discover they have little say as to the direction of the CCRC.

Typical complaints center on building and expansion plans based on questionable financial projections and leveraged operations that use income from one facility to operate, build or expand at other facilities.

Residents are not automatically entitled to be on the CCRC's board of directors or even attend their meetings.

There are concerns that residents would not approve any increases or modernization programs because they want a minimum monthly fee and aren't concerned about the future success of the CCRC.

That should change as more baby boomers enter CCRCs.

Previous CCRC generations were heavily loaded with ministry/missionary retirees, given that so many CCRCs were started by religious groups. It was common, and still is at some older CCRCs, for dinner to be served boardinghouse style by passing plates around the dining table.

Today, more corporate baby boomers are entering CCRCs, and they understand the need to invest and grow communities. (You can tell the baby boomers have arrived if there's an executive chef.)

Years ago, the CCRC executive director probably was a retired minister who may have had a PhD in religious studies but only an elementary understanding of finances and marketing. Today, it would be difficult to get a job as an executive director without an MBA or similar degree.

It's a minority of CCRCs, however, that have residents as board members and an even smaller subset that have residents as full voting members. Baby boomers may not accept the autocratic management of single site executive directors.

I'm constantly reading articles about CCRCs working on facility improvements to entice baby boomers but haven't seen issues of governance addressed.

I don't think baby boomers will put up with the type of autocratic management the older passive ministry/missionary group did.

At a minimum, all board meetings except for personnel issues should be open to residents.

Residents moving out

I couldn't find any studies on why residents leave CCRCs; this is something the industry doesn't want to fund.

Based on my experience over the past decade, I've seen people leave for one of three reasons:

1) they want to be nearer family;
2) they want lower fees or
3) they don't agree with the way the CCRC is managed.

Every single (live!) resident I've seen leave has been for one of those three reasons.

Bottomline

Baby boomers may drive CCRCs toward more condominium style of management with residents serving on the board of directors and having a vote in the future of the community.

Examine the Financial Stability of the CCRC

The best advice I can give you is to get three to five years' worth of financial statements from the CCRC.

Those statements should include a balance sheet showing the assets and liabilities of the CCRC and an income statement showing profit and loss as well as three years of the IRS Form 990, Return of Organization Exempt from Income Tax Filings which is submitted annually (see next chapter).

If you don't have an accounting background, have an accountant or financial planner examine the records for you. S/he may have questions for you to take to the CCRC treasurer.

So much of your future satisfaction is tied to living in a financially strong CCRC. I really hope you will take this bit of advice even if you ignore everything else I suggest!

In the meantime, there are certain items you could examine for yourself.

What is the occupancy rate?

The best choice is a community that's 90% or more full. I would avoid a community that's below 85% full.

That indicates the community may not be attracting the newcomers and their entrance fees that it needs for capital improvements or routine maintenance.

People rarely move into CCRCs on a day's notice. They usually sell their homes or cash out investments which can take time and may be difficult in a poor economic environment.

Keep in mind, once a CCRC occupancy rate slips below 80%, it is very, very challenging to obtain enough new residents to maintain the cash flow the CCRC needs to operate.

The best CCRCs have waiting lists. Find out what the occupancy rate has been for each of the past three years.

You also should ask how many residents move out of the CCRC each year.

Does incoming cash flow exceed operating costs?

If the answer is no, you need to understand how the shortage is covered.

Is there any chance the CCRC will close or merge with another community if the shortage continues?

Is the community relying on donations and endowments to survive? That's very risky.

In a mature CCRC, the ratio of cash to debt should be around 35 percent.

It's not unusual for a new CCRC to have a negative net worth (liabilities exceed assets), which is not overly concerning as long as they have a steady stream of income from residents, new and existing.

How much cash does it have on hand?

Cash on hand means how many days the CCRC could continue to operate if no resident paid a cent.

Based on filings with the state insurance department, the average Florida nonprofit CCRC had enough liquid cash to operate 180 days without receiving anything from any resident.

CCRCs traditionally averaged 182 days cash on hand; however, the total average was based on 59 days for for-profit and 218 days for nonprofit CCRCs.

How is it marketing to baby boomers?

Older CCRCs were designed like apartment complexes and often had no garages or even covered parking.

There were small kitchens and they often lacked any laundry facility in the unit.

That style won't fly with today's baby boomer.

Many want slightly smaller homes but granite or quartz kitchen countertops, stainless steel appliances including an icemaker in the refrigerator door, garages, and unit washer and dryers.

They'd also better have a good fitness center and wellness program.

Some of the newer CCRCs are going to a cluster style of living for assisted living.

Instead of long hallways and central dining areas, the clusters have a communal kitchen and living area with private bedrooms and bathrooms. Some seniors find this a homier environment.

If the CCRC is not building or has not built homes to appeal to this new demographic group of retirees, the community may run into trouble maintaining occupancy rates.

What are the building plans for the next three to five years?

Even if the CCRC has no space to build new facilities, every physical plant will require periodic renovations. What is the community's plan for the next major improvements and how will they pay for it?

How much long-term debt does it have and how is it paying it off?

Building these baby boomer homes is not cheap. The CCRC should be using entrance fees and/or bond issues to fund construction.

If the CCRC has bond financing, find out how long the community will be paying off the bonds.

One good aspect of long-term debt is that to get it the CCRC probably had to have 300 days of cash on hand and a minimum of 25 percent cash to debt ratio.

I would expect the entrance fees to be used for construction or other long-term debt and the monthly fee to be used for operating costs.

Does the community have a reserve fund? If so, how are the funds used?

Ideally, the CCRC should not have to use reserves for immediate operating costs or things like marketing.

Reserves should be for unplanned events, such as repair of a water main break or to cover insurance policy deductions.

If the community has a residents' council, is the council apprised of how expenses and reserves are being spent and does the residents' council have any oversight on how CCRC finances are managed?

How often are monthly fees increased and what is the basis for the increase?

Your contract should state how often fees may be increased and how notice is given. For instance, fees may be increased once a year with 30- or 60-days' written notice.

Some CCRCs will tie the increase to an inflation rate or index or match the increase in social security benefits. Ask about this and see how logical the rationale for increases sounds to you.

Typical increases for the past few years range from 2 to 5 percent.

Any increase in one year over 5% should be a red flag. Understand why that happened.

If the CCRC is one of a chain, see if a parent group or all the communities share financial responsibility.

The typical response will be that they do not. Each CCRC usually is a separate entity that is responsible for its own debts, but there may be some sharing of costs or a contingency fund that all the communities share.

Be concerned if all the CCRCs are responsible for one another's losses and shortfalls.

Has the CCRC been involved in any lawsuits?

Do a Google search or ask your lawyer to search for you. As an example, one well-known Texas CCRC was successfully sued after a resident swallowed a corrosive cleaning compound that had been placed in a water jug.

RUTH ALVAREZ

Unfortunately, the CCRC had been on the losing end of a recent similar lawsuit and the jury returned a seven-figure verdict against the CCRC for punitive damages.

If you find something similar, ask the CCRC about the costs and potential impacts of a future resident's fees and services. What is management doing to prevent recurrences?

Bottomline

Review your finances and the CCRC's finances with competent professionals before you sign any contract.

Internal Revenue Service (IRS) Form 990

Organizations with an IRS 501(c)(3) non-profit status (most nonprofit CCRCs) are required to file a Form 990, *Return of Organizations Exempt from Income Tax* with the IRS.

Any professional financial or accounting person you use to examine potential CCRCs should want to see these. Even if you don't use a professional, you should look at them yourself.

How to obtain a copy

IRS Form 990 is a public record and, under IRS regulations, a non-profit is required to make the last three years of the Form 990 available to the public upon request either by mail, electronic document, website, or at its principal office.

Form 990 is a valuable look into CCRC candidates. The IRS website has a copy and explanation of the data required at **http://www.irs.gov/pub/irs-pdf/i990.pdf**.

An independent resource for non-profit CCRCs, ProPublica offers a "Nonprofit Explorer" tool that includes financial information from prior and current years gathered from Form 990s at **https://projects.propublica.org/nonprofits**.

If your CCRC is part of a chain, you may need to search by overall corporate owner. Also, this tool does not include for-profit CCRCs.

Key items for review

1. Examine reports for a two or three year period to observe trends and any data fields left blank.

2. Part I Summary shows total revenue and total expenses, and total assets and liabilities. It is a statement of the organization's positive or negative net worth.

3. Part III describes new services and services terminated. It also lists the three largest services measured by expenses, expenditures, grants and revenues.

4. Part VII and Schedule J list compensation of board members, executive director and other top management as well as employees earning over $100,000.

Look especially at the board's and director's salaries for the three years. If there have been significant changes, I'd want to know why and whether there was any change in responsibilities.

5. Schedule D provides information on donor and endowment funds.

6. Schedule K reveals if the CCRC has issued tax-exempt bonds.

7. If you're interested in a multi-site CCRC, check out Schedule R for the amounts and types of transactions for the specific CCRC in relation to the multi facility parent and any subsidiaries.

Bottomline

Form 990 is a valuable look into CCRC candidates. The IRS website has a copy and explanation of the data required at
http://www.irs.gov/pub/irs-pdf/i990.pdf.

Bankruptcy — Part I: Recession

The senior housing market was rocked in 2009 when Erickson Retirement Communities, at that time the largest chain of senior communities in the USA, filed for Chapter 11 bankruptcy protection, claiming more than $1 billion in both assets and liabilities.

Erickson's situation (oversimplified):

Erickson developed and built CCRCs as a for-profit corporation and then operated the CCRCs as nonprofits.

With 23,000 residents in more than a dozen states, the company was successful and profitable for a long period of time.

Unfortunately, the company kept adding communities, but the housing market tanked, which made it difficult for potential residents to sell their homes and pay the entrance fees. Bank credit markets tightened cash reserve requirements, and it became impossible for Erickson to ride out the recession.

Although there was a foreclosure on one new facility (which had no residents), the existing communities today are run by nonprofits overseen by National Senior Campuses, and no Erickson residents lost their entrance fee.

I have a good friend who still lives in one of the Erickson communities. She, along with all her neighbors, was worried when the bankruptcy occurred and wondered if they'd start getting bologna sandwiches for dinner.

Fortunately, the impact was minimal for residents. Erickson immediately stopped all construction on a new part of the complex, but the rest of the community operated as usual.

In fact, she had more complaints when the housing market rebounded, and Erickson started building and selling units again. In her opinion, the infrastructure didn't keep with up the pace of new residents.

Erickson wasn't alone

Many communities, profit and nonprofit, have experienced problems because of recession, pandemic close down, inflation, competition and seniors who retrofit their homes for long-term stay rather than move to retirement communities.

The well-known for-profit Sunrise Senior Living Inc. sold off 21 of its assisted living communities after losing more than $80M.

The Archdiocese of Philadelphia sold seven senior living communities to a for-profit group.

Other communities that have experienced financial difficulties were St. Mary of the Woods in Avon, OH; Village at Penn State in Ambler, PA; Querencia at Barton Creek in Austin, TX; Fairview Village in Downers Grove, IL; River Terrace Estates in Bluffton, IN; and Devonshire at PGA National in Palm Beach Gardens, FA.

Other well-publicized communities filing for Chapter 11 bankruptcy protection included Sears Methodist Retirement Communities; The Edgemere in Dallas (where entrance fees could exceed $1M); Mirador in Corpus Christi, TX; The Buckingham in Houston; Stayton at Museum Way in Fort Worth; and The Franciscan Sisters of Chicago with a 53-story Chicago building.

Only one community lost all entrance fees.

Covenant at South Hills in Lebanon Hills, PA, was almost ten years old before it entered bankruptcy.

It never reached its projected occupancy levels before it was faced with the troubled housing market including tight credit.

A major problem for it was the fact that the local tax assessor had overturned the community's property tax-exempt status. Not only did Covenant have to pay property taxes, it also had to pay a penalty of more than $3 million.

Once Covenant filed for bankruptcy, residents were shocked to discover that their right to entrance fee refunds was subordinate to lender liens. Essentially, they were unsecured creditors in a bankruptcy and had no legal right to receive anything.

Concordia Lutheran Ministries of Pittsburgh later bought the community, renamed it Concordia of the South Hills, and continued the residents' life care contracts.

About 100 residents, however, are suing the previous owner, B'nai B'rith Housing, a nonprofit affiliate of B'nai B'rith International, to recoup their entrance fees.

Bottom line

The best advice I could ever offer you is to get professional help to analyze a community's financial position.

Sadly, things still can change. We have seen problems arise both in longstanding and new communities, both for-profit and nonprofit communities.

But keep reading.

Bankruptcy — Part II: Present

We can understand financial difficulties during a recession, but how do you explain what's happened in Florida post-recession and pandemic?

One of the CCRCs, a nonprofit, restructured via bankruptcy court and continues to operate.

A second CCRC was taken over by Erickson Living and continues to operate.

The third, a for-profit community, is still in bankruptcy court and is discussed in detail further on.

It's noteworthy that the luxury CCRC Erickson acquired had defaulted on its $158.2 million mortgage.

That CCRC had been acquired by a private equity group in 2007 when it had a beautiful campus, a 97% occupancy rate and entrance fees between $222,000 and $687,000.

As mentioned in the previous chapter, the entrance fees residents pay are unsecured debt during a bankruptcy. That means residents are at the end of the line (behind the court, lawyers, and secured creditors) for refunds.

The CCRCs that get in trouble usually use entrance fees to support operating costs because few states require CCRCs to keep a portion of entrance fees available for refunds.

Nonprofits may not worry when liabilities exceed assets, but with for-profit businesses, that often causes a financial reorganization.

CCRC in Tampa, FL

One of the largest bankruptcies occurred at a CCRC in beautiful Tampa, FL.

For more than two years, the 500 residents there had been living with the anxiety of not knowing what's going to happen to the community and losing hope that they'll ever recoup any funding.

The state insurance office estimated the CCRC owes more than $4 million in entrance fee refunds.

Some of the key items contributing to the financial breakdown, according to a Florida state investigation, included:

- Selling the community to a private equity group without state approval;
- Operating without obtaining the required state licenses and certifications;
- Entering into contracts with family members and friends at unreasonable fees;
- Contracting management services to someone who'd been involved with a bankruptcy at an assisted living facility the year before;
- Failing to pay vendors;
- Failing to pay employees' medical insurance premiums even though money was taken from employee paychecks;
- Issuing employee paychecks with insufficient funds; and

- Continuing to accept new residents even though the CCRC was technically bankrupt.

The state of Florida sued the owners who spent whatever funds they had fighting the state rather than maintaining the facility.

Residents still living there complained that there was no air conditioning in the dining room during the summer and no heat in the dining room during the winter. At one point, residents had to wear coats to the dining room where the temperature only reached 51-degrees.

Residents dealt with trash dumpsters that sat full for months with an odor of rotting garbage, backed-up sewage and broken elevators.

Finally, the hard-pressed residents had to hire their own lawyer to represent them at bankruptcy court.

There was no happy ending for the residents. Although a new company took ownership, they could not turnaround the community which was only 20% occupied when it closed. Residents were forced to move out.

Political segue (read at your own risk)

As a result of these bankruptcies, Florida legislators introduced legislation to help prevent similar Tampa problems. The laws provide more transparency in CCRC operations and allow the state to step in sooner when problems arise.

The laws proposed would not be as encompassing and protective of residents without the lobbying and advocacy of FLiCRA, the Florida Life Care Residents Association (see **http://www.flicra.com/**).

I cannot overstate the importance of this group to the welfare of CCRC residents.

If your state has a similar organization, you need to participate.

We also benefited from the support of then-Governor Rick Scott's office and AARP.

Although AARP's first allegiance is always to protect the affiliate fees it gets from UnitedHealthcare, in this case there was no threat to its money machine so it worked to support CCRC residents.

As I noted, this section may offend some people, but group lobbying and having prominent advocates is the only way to enact laws that protect seniors.

For example, the private equity group that owned the Tampa facility has been accused of siphoning off millions of dollars to enrich its investors at the expense of the residents and employees of the CCRC.

Equity groups may be suspect (I really want to say 'evil'), but they're not poor.

They're going to spend money to lobby legislators, hire lawyers and publicists, and protect their interests.

You need to organize by joining FLiCRA or equivalent state groups and enlist all the supportive politicians you can.

Bottom line

Reread the chapter **Examine the Financial Stability of the CCRC** and have a financial or accounting professional review the CCRC's audited records.

It's never a bad idea to have an experienced lawyer, especially an elder law specialist, review the contract.

If a private equity group owns the CCRC, be especially wary.

Storm Clouds at the CCRC

Besides the economic pressures, there are four forces that have a disparately negative impact on CCRCs.

Staffing needs outweigh every other problem

The most pressing concern for CCRCs will be hiring enough staff of sufficient quality and training to provide the type of care state and federal governments demand for certifications and residents demand for themselves.

These jobs have traditionally not paid well while being physically and emotionally demanding.

Well managed CCRCs are making efforts to reward length of service and to fund advanced training for staff so employees can see a potential future with increased pay and status.

Artificial Intelligence (AI) is starting to invade the senior care communities but is currently used mostly in meal preparation and dining room functions.

Japanese manufacturers have been working on robotic aids that can care for the elderly. Someday we may have human-like robots in nursing facilities.

Sometimes communities use private nursing services or employment agencies to staff their facilities. These staff often include foreign nationals.

Some countries, such as the Philippines, are known for well educated nursing employees, and the quality of care may be more than satisfactory.

The likely problem, however, is that staff may not be able to communicate well in English. That's especially problematic for frail and ill seniors and dementia patients. Social interaction is a necessity for these residents and not being able to understand staff (and vice versus) is a huge problem.

Using staffing agencies also is expensive for CCRCs.

I expect to see more CCRCs reduce the number of Skilled Nursing Facility (SNF) beds in their communities as high staffing costs and shortages coupled with politically volatile reimbursement rates make it economically difficult to maintain required quality.

You also can expect to see some CCRCs eschew SNFs altogether and use more assisted living and memory care facilities to handle frail residents.

Alternatively, they may no longer offer SNF or memory care services and encourage residents to use hospitals and facilities run by other groups. This also greatly reduces the CCRC's liability risk for medical care.

Remember, the federal government regulates SNFs while states cover assisted living. CCRCs have much more flexibility in staff ratios (caregiver to patient) in independent and assisted living.

See tips in the Touring chapter to address this.

Government reimbursement rates continue to decline

Reimbursement is a four-letter word to CCRC management. Governments, federal and state, have reduced funding and reimbursement in Medicare and Medicaid.

The Patient Protection and Affordable Care Act, more popularly known as Obamacare, reduced Medicare funding and Medicare reimbursement rates to help pay for Obamacare.

As an example, Medicare home health care suffered a total 14% reduction.

Additionally, Medicaid is the single most frequent payer of skilled nursing facility (SNF) patient. Medicaid is a part federal/part state program and reimbursement rates take a hit from both government bodies.

Even nonprofits have been forced to close SNFs because states reduced their portion of reimbursement rates.

People are living longer but with more physical limitations

The average age of a newcomer to a CCRC has risen from the 70s to the 80s. A typical newcomer is between 80 to 83 years of age – if not older.

Residents also enter assisted living today with an average of more than 14 chronic conditions while new residents at CCRCs or life plan communities averaged 12 chronic conditions.

Of course, not all conditions are grave. Chronic conditions include low thyroid, high cholesterol, vision loss, osteoporosis, and hearing loss as well as more serious and expensive to treat conditions such as dementia, heart disease, type 2 diabetes, and arthritis.

That reflects the facts that people are living longer than they used to and that today's 80-year-old is better educated and has more support options (mechanical, medical, and technological) than an 80-year-old of a decade ago.

More people are living to be 100 than ever before and this trend is likely to continue (baring nuclear war, etc.). According to the U. S. Census Bureau, the number of Americans over 100 years of age doubled between 1990 and 2010. That level of growth is expected to continue if not accelerate.

At the same time, some life care communities may not be ready for this. When people moved in 20 years ago, the actuarial tables used to determine the entrance fee may not have assumed 40 more years of life expectancy.

Our point here is not to have a philosophical discussion on the merits of extending life for people with debilitating diseases or long-term care in general, but rather to point out the financial burden this places on long existing CCRCs.

These communities are going have a large number of frail seniors while they are trying to entice active younger residents into their community.

CCRCs older than 10 years tend to have a majority of residents between the ages of 85 and 87, according to US News Health.

Unlike some businesses, the fact a CCRC has been in existence a long time may be as much a negative as a positive. You must—YOU MUST—examine the financial soundness of any CCRC you consider and it is worth paying an accountant to do that for you.

Unfortunately, very few CCRCs have an actuary (a professional who analyzes financial consequences of risk) on their board of directors, but someone needs to be looking at this for the community.

People are suing more

Any CCRC may be sued. Remember when a woman got a $1 million for spilling hot coffee on herself while driving? People sue for anything and get ridiculous awards.

A risk consultant company working with the American Health Care Association estimated liability costs for long-term care providers increase by 5% a year with a typical loss rate of $2,030 per occupied bed.

The typical loss, of course, varies greatly by location. For instance, Kentucky, at the time of the study, had the highest rate in the nation with average of $9,220 per occupied bed.

That means a Kentucky nursing home with 100 beds would have an annual liability cost of $922,000. That will be amortized into the fees the residents pay. On the other hand, Texas nursing homes average less than $1,000 per occupied bed.

Is the care in Texas so much better than Kentucky? Doubtful. What is different is that Kentucky is a plaintiff lawyer-friendly state while Texas has tort reform and limits on non-economic damages.

Equally important to just the rise in lawsuits is the impact of Americans with Disabilities Act (ADA) and Fair Housing Act lawsuits to change who is allowed to live in independent housing.

Will these laws allow CCRCs to force a senior to move from independence living into assisted living or will a CCRC be forced to provide these services in independent living?

ADA requires 'reasonable accommodation' for people so they may use and enjoy their place of residency. What constitutes 'reasonable' is up to individual judges and juries.

A California court permitted a CCRC to transfer a 13-year resident to assisted living from independent living.

The resident had sued to stop the transfer, but the court sided with the CCRC because her care needs—hygiene, dressing and grooming— exceeded those that California law allows to be provided in independent living.

In another highly publicized case where the AARP assisted the resident in bringing a lawsuit, the CCRC settled out of court and allowed the resident to remain in independent living with additional care.

In a recent Michigan case, the medical staff of a CCRC was not allowed to evaluate whether a resident returning from a hospital stay was able to live independently.

On the other hand, there is no liability relief to the CCRC if the resident falls or injures himself because he wasn't able to function on his own.

There's also no financial help to enable a CCRC to staff independent living as heavily as assisted living.

There's also never a concern for neighbors who live next door to someone who may be a danger to himself or the community. (This is another reason why should never buy into a community that has gas stovetops or ovens in its living units.)

Bottomline

Stay healthy!

Who Regulates CCRCs?

Government regulations

CCRCs generally are regulated by state rather than federal government.

A 2023 federal Government Accounting Office study found that 38 states have some level of regulation specifically addressing CCRCs.

On the other hand, 12 states and the District of Columbia do not.

The states without specific CCRC regulations (as of this writing) are Alabama, Alaska, Colorado, Hawaii, Mississippi, Montana, Nebraska, Nevada, North Dakota, South Dakota, Utah, and West Virginia.

Of the states that regulate CCRCs, there is a wide variation in the degree of regulation.

For instance, Connecticut only requires CCRCs to submit annual financial and insurance information while California, Florida and New York require more extensive evaluations and issue operating certificates.

Level of housing

Independent living usually is regulated the same as single or multifamily housing in the community through zoning and building codes.

There are guidelines from the Americans with Disabilities Act (ADA), such as levers to open cabinets that senior housing usually implements.

States have more rules and oversight for assisted living but, again, enforcement may be minimal.

The federal government becomes a significant player for Medicare and Medicaid in the SNF.

There are many regulations for a facility to qualify for Medicaid, and it's desirable to find a CCRC where the nursing facility is certified even if you never plan to make use of it.

Bottomline

Don't assume the state is protecting you. Due diligence in selecting a CCRC is crucial.

What Accreditations or Certifications Should You Look For?

People considering CCRCs often limit their search to communities with specific accreditations or certifications.

Outside of Medicare and Medicaid, that sounds better than it really is. I would not cross off a community only because it lacks CARF or other certification for the reasons described in the following.

CARF - Commission on Accreditation of Rehabilitation Facilities

CARF is a nonprofit group that accredits CCRC (and other types of) communities. Sophisticated baby boomers often start looking for a member community by using the provider search tool on the **CARF-CCAC** (Continuing Care Accreditation Commission) **http://www.carf.org/providerSearch.aspx** website.

CCRCs are evaluated both through submittal of financial data and operating plans as well as an on-site visit. Accreditation may be for one to three years, and there is a substantial fee for CCRCs to request accreditation. It is a voluntary undertaking.

It's not unheard of for a new CCRC to obtain accreditation for marketing purposes and then let the accreditation expire once they are operating at or near full capacity because the cost of obtaining it is no longer of benefit.

Many CCRCs have been operating long enough and have such a good reputation that most new residents come from the area in which the CCRC is located or from referrals of existing residents.

Quakers (Religious Society of Friends) operate some CCRCs with excellent reputations on the East Coast but they don't bother, or need to, spend the money to obtain CARF accreditation.

The reason I don't think CARF accreditation should be a deal breaker is that CARF does not disclose in any detail how the accreditation is determined and some data and evaluation is self-reported by the CCRC.

CARF accreditation is good and even necessary for a new CCRC.

I would not, however, cross off a CCRC over five years of age only because it doesn't have CARF accreditation.

American Health Care Association and National Center for Assisted Living (AHCA/NCAL)

This is a nonprofit group whose members provide long-term care to elderly and disabled individuals.

It provides annual Bronze, Silver or Gold awards (like the Olympics) to facilities based on an evaluation of the quality of their processes and operation.

The top-tier Gold award recipients must also complete the rigorous Baldrige Criteria for Performance Excellence in Health Care.

Similar to CARF-CCAC, communities must apply and pay a fee for the evaluation. Unlike CARF-CCAC, this group is more open about their evaluation criteria and what they expect for each award. I like the fact that one of their key measurements is staff turnover.

Resources for Consumers (ahcancal.org)

Medicaid certification

Check the **Medicare.gov** website to find a nursing home provider. I recommend selecting one that is certified to accept Medicaid as well as Medicare.

If you're in a SNF that doesn't accept Medicaid, you could be moved to a less desirable facility if you run out of money.

You also could be moved to another facility, if the beds targeted for Medicaid are filled with none available when you need one. This is one of the points to discuss before you sign a contract.

Each listed home is given one to five stars based on health inspections, staffing and quality measures. The kicker is that facilities themselves provide the data to evaluate staffing and quality measures, although health inspections are performed by outside trained inspectors.

Joint Commission

An independent, nonprofit organization known as the Joint Commission accredits or certifies more than 19,000 SNFs and other health care facilities including hospitals.

It has a long list of standards that facilities must meet to obtain certification. This is one of the most rigorous of the evaluation groups.

To apply for accreditation, the SNF must pay a fee and have an on-site evaluation by Joint Commission staff.

The Joint Commission also offers a Memory Care Certification program developed in collaboration with the Alzheimer's Association.

The organization's highest award is the Joint Commission's Gold Seal of Approval. You can visit the **Joint Commission.org** website to search for accredited providers or go to **https://www.qualitycheck.org**.

Financial scores

If your CCRC has or is offering bonds for sale to finance development, the CCRC bonds will have a rating from **Fitch Ratings**, **Moodys** or **Standard & Poor**.

Ratings typically range from AAA to C with the more the As, the better.

It's worthwhile to read the explanation that goes along with the ratings, and occupancy rates are a key measure.

All three allow you to search for ratings on their websites, although Fitch's and Moody's require free registration.

Nonprofit assets

An easy way to get a snapshot of a nonprofit CCRC is to visit **Nonprofit Explorer - ProPublica (https://projects.propublica.org/nonprofits/)**. You'll see revenue, expenses, assets and liabilities as reported on IRS documents.

The only downside is you must know the precise name of your facility on IRS reports. For example, Five Pines CCRC may actually be Northern States Retirement Home of the Pentevangelica Society of America.

State certifications

Check your state's senior services and see if a state agency provides ratings or certifications on senior facilities.

Also check at **https://eldercare.acl.gov/Public/Search_Results.aspx** for the local Area Agency for Aging in your city and state.

For example, the Florida Governor's Panel on Excellence in Long-Term Care recognizes nursing homes with high standards and high quality of care with a Gold Seal Award. Criteria to obtain a Gold Seal include staff turnover rates, best practices, consumer satisfaction ratings, community involvement and financial stability.

Slightly fewer than 20 of Florida's 682 SNFs have received this award.

For-profit communities

Website **mylifesite.net** has general information on CCRCs and some specific information on many, but not all, CCRCs in at least 12 states. It's worth looking at what they have.

Bottomline

I would avoid any CCRC that doesn't have a Medicare/Medicaid certified SNF but other certifications are data points but not probative.

Taking the Tour

Many CCRCs will offer you a free night or two stay, and that's a good way to explore the community without a marketing person constantly being underfoot.

Make at least three to four visits to a community before you decide it's the one. Try to stay for dinner (marketing people usually go home after 5 p.m.) and meet more residents.

If the community has functions open to the general public, participate and try to talk to as many residents as possible.

Initial planning

Decide on acceptable locations. Look at CCRC and senior housing websites and then call for information.

Ask about entrance and monthly fees, whether they accept pets (assuming you have one) and if they have the type of housing you want (apartment or duplex or single-family home, whatever plus a garage).

Those things will weed out lots of candidates.

Ask for brochures from the CCRCs that are still on the list.

Don't

Don't try to look at 200 items and don't put things like 'Olympic swimming pool' on your list if you don't swim and don't want to learn.

Don't focus on easily corrected items.

- You can have grab bars installed in the shower or toilet area.

- You can replace the refrigerator with one that has an ice maker in the door.
- You can repaint the bedroom.

Do

Think long and hard about the location you want and need.

Look at the facilities you can't easily or inexpensively change.

Pick no more than ten items that really mean something to you and see if they're available at or near that location.

Eat in the dining room a couple times and see if you like the food, if the dining room seems well managed (enough staff, they aren't running out of basic items, and hot food is hot, cold food is cold) and if other residents are friendly.

Consider how easy or difficult it is to reach the dining area, wellness center and main building from the living areas. You don' t want to have to walk outside in the open when it's raining, snowing or too dark.

Do you feel safe making the walk? I don't mean fear of getting mugged but fear of falling if there are no railings, too many steep steps or uneven elevations that would challenge someone with a walker.

Notice if there are separate dining rooms for independent vs assisted living vs nursing/memory care residents. That might be an important point if you're a couple and one person eventually moves to a different level of care.

Try to meet the people who would be living next door and see if you think you'd be a good fit.

Narrow the candidates

Once you've visited several candidates, verify the financial soundness and accreditation (such as Medicare and Medicaid eligibility) of the subset that really interest you.

You should have a shortlist of no more than half a dozen communities.

If you have more than six, you don't know yourself well enough and need to do a little more soul-searching.

Have your accountant or financial planner check out the financial statements. Review the CCRC contract and handbook for residents.

Then go with your gut instinct.

Here are some tips to help you winnow down the list.

Look at the surrounding area

Obviously, you don't want a high crime or run-down area. If you have a dog, is there a safe area to walk him?

What's not so obvious is that there may be no public transportation nearby or you are 90 minutes away from a shopping mall. You may or may not care about those things.

If you have family or friends who will visit you, how easy will it be for them to reach the CCRC? Is there a nearby airport? Are there housing and parking for guests?

Are there activities or amusement areas around that can accommodate visiting grandchildren? If you're 10 miles from Disney World or similar, you can expect frequent visits as compared to being four hours from any major urban center.

Is it important to you to have a natural or health foods store in the area? Are there other types of stores that you want close by?

If you are devoted to certain hobbies or interests, are there groups or facilities readily available for you?

I've lost count of how many people have told me they love living in The Villages in Florida because there are special interest groups for every and all interests and backgrounds. (Too bad, The Villages isn't a CCRC, just a huge retirement community.)

Are there certain types of restaurants, e.g., vegan or Asian, that you insist be nearby?

Again, you must understand what's important to you and see if it exists there.

How far are you from medical facilities?

Is there a local hospital and long would it take to get you there in an emergency?

At the minimum, you should consider where you could receive treatment and follow-up care in the event of stroke, heart attack and cancer—the three huge threats for seniors.

It will not be pleasant to drive four hours each way to get treatment.

Is there more than one hospital in town or nearby?

If one hospital or doctor's clinic stops taking Medicare or your supplemental insurance, what would you do?

As mentioned before, will you be able to get surgical after care and rehabilitation within your community?

I can't stress enough how much easier your recovery is if you don't have to continually travel for care.

Look at how well-kept the grounds and buildings are throughout the community

Don't focus on architecture or landscape design. You'll get used to them.

See instead if things are being kept up, especially the grounds.

If the CCRC is becoming financially strapped, facility and grounds upkeep is often one of the first things to suffer.

Are the facilities clean and do they smell clean. Check the top of the door into the dining room or wellness center. Look at vents to see if they're dusted.

Look for security measures

Is there a guard gate if it's a gated community? Are there security cameras or security guards on duty at night? Do residents use a security service such as ADT?

If you had an emergency, is there an easily reached call button in your living unit or on your person?

Does the community have a system to check on its residents? For instance, a relative lived in a community where residents had to place a magnetic sign on their front door by 10 p.m. every day and remove it by 10 a.m.

Security would visit any residence that didn't meet that criteria and hadn't let management know the resident wouldn't be home.

Ask about emergency preparedness

Many areas, especially coastal areas, are subject to severe weather. What is the community's evacuation plan?

Power failures also are a common occurrence throughout the U.S. Does the community have generators in independent living and assisted living or at least in some common areas? Will the kitchen and dining room be able to continue serving residents?

Many states and the federal government require emergency electrical power for Skilled Nursing Facilities. Ask if that includes air conditioning and heating for resident rooms as well as electrical power for life support equipment, hallways and elevators.

See if the marketing people let you eat a meal without them

Going by yourself to the cafeteria or dining room is a good way to meet other residents without someone from the community putting a damper on the conversation.

The residents who are eating there also are apt to be the more social ones and are likely to welcome giving their opinion on the CCRC.

Tell them you're a visitor and ask if you can pick their brains on the CCRC.

This is also a good way to get a feel for the types of people who live there.

If you're a single male, look around and see how many other single males you see at meals. There won't be many, since women outnumber men at all CCRCs. You'd want at least a few.

Look for the activities you want

If you play pickleball, is there a pickleball court and have you ever seen anyone using it during your visits?

See if the community has a room or equipment that supports the type of activities you like to do.

Be sure to get copies of the current and previous month's activities calendar.

Check out the noise level and how it's contained

Try to visit someone who's living there and see how noisy their home or apartment is.

If you're going into an apartment or otherwise will share a wall with a neighbor and are sensitive to noise, take a friend with you.

If the apartment next door is vacant, have your friend run water and flush a toilet there and see if you hear it in your prospective apartment.

If you can't get into the unit(s) surrounding you, at least have your friend flush a toilet in your unit or talk in a back room and see how the sound carries to the living room where you are.

Ask the marketing representative how the community handles noise complaints. There are always near-deaf people who turn on their TVs too loud but refuse to get hearing aids. The community should have a protocol to address this.

If the complex wasn't designed and built to minimize noise between neighbors, you could spend a lot of money and suffer much aggravation trying to ameliorate that.

Greet as many staff members as possible

Are they friendly? Do they look like they're engaged by their work? Are they doing a good job?

Ask staff who they work for. Ideally, the answer will be the community. If it's a staffing agency, ask the community how difficult it is for them to hire and how they recruit potential new employees.

Do you see signs or special parking places for "Employees of the Month" or similar? Is there a bulletin board or other areas just for employees?

When you're in the buildings, are the staff speaking in English or a language you understand? This doesn't matter with the ground maintenance crew but may be a problem with nursing and support staff.

People need to communicate with others to feel connected to the ongoing world.

Tour the entire community including assisted living and SNF

Read the next chapters on those and then see what you think of those facilities.

Look at the living arrangements. In older church-based communities, it was not uncommon for assisted living units to offer dual occupancy and for an SNF to have as many as four occupants to a room.

If you step into the SNF and it reeks of urine or residents are listlessly sitting in wheelchairs around the nurses' station while aids talk on their cellphones, go to the next name on your list.

Additional Tips for Assisted Living (AL), Skilled Nursing Facilities (SNF) and Memory Care

Do not avoid a tour of these facilities just because you are moving into independent living and think an SNF is a long, long way off.

You never know what might happen (stroke, auto accident, kidney failure, etc.) and how well the CCRC treats its most vulnerable residents will tell you a lot about how seriously they treat their great-sounding mission statement.

Ask how many rooms/beds they have in each type of facility and how many in SNF are Medicaid beds.

The latter question is crucial. Many SNFs only allot a limited number of beds for Medicaid patients (because the government reimbursement is so low).

For any but a Type A contract, CCRC residents typically pay the market rate for SNFs until theyv'e expended all private funds and then Medicaid picks up the cost.

Will the CCRC let you stay and have the benevolence fund pick up the tab? Do they have the right, per your contract, to move you to a lower cost SNF, within your CCRC community if you're in a chain ownership or without if you're not.

What do the residents do all day?

Find out what activities are offered and how frequently the residents are taken on outings. Ask to see the monthly calendar of events for the past three months.

At some CCRCs, the independent living residents have a social calendar that would tax Paris Hilton while the AL and SNF residents are offered a 40-year-old movie in the projector room once a month.

Find out if AL and SNF residents are permitted, even encouraged, to take advantage of the activities in independent living such as outings and tours and if they don't have their own events.

Are volunteers encouraged to come by and help residents with activities?

When you visit the SNF, make sure to visit the nurses' station.

- Are residents just sitting around the station all day?
- Do the residents look clean, well groomed, and well fed?
- Have the female residents had the back of their hair combed? (Most AL residents find it difficult to reach back there and that's a task that understaffed ALs rarely have time to do.)

What types of staff are there?

A Medicare and Medicaid-certified SNF will be required to have a certain number of trained staff and meet numerous requirements.

Currently, rules require a registered nurse (RN) director of nursing, an RN on duty at least 8 hours a day, 7 days a week and an RN or licensed practical nurse (LPN) on duty the rest of the time.

The AL unit, however, is regulated by the state and sometimes quite minimally. The ratio of staff to residents sounds like a good measure but so much depends on the number and types of patients, such as whether there are dementia patients.

More importantly, even if the staffing is at a high level (example, one aide to five residents), the facility may not have temporary staffing available to fill in when someone is on vacation or calls in sick. That's not unusual especially for night duty.

In all cases, there should be a registered nurse or physician available on call 24/7.

Ask about the skill level of caregivers, especially for AL.

They may have nothing more than the CCRC's own orientation or they may be Certified Nursing Assistants (CNAs) or Licensed Practical Nurse (LPNs). What duties they may perform are controlled by your state and the facility.

CNAs may have 75 hours of training (the minimum required for Medicare/Medicaid) or three to six months of training/certification, depending on state laws.

CNAs help with personal care as well as uncomplicated medical chores like taking temperatures.

LPNs are usually licensed by the state and complete up to two years of vocational training. They perform nursing duties under the supervision of a doctor and are higher paid than CNAs.

It's the CNAs, however, that make-or-break resident satisfaction at SNFs. See how the CCRC treats its staff and ask about CNA turnover.

These are relatively low-paid, high responsibility jobs and burnout is endemic.

What type of therapies are offered?

Find out what types of therapies are offered and whether pets are allowed. The latter can be a major issue for devoted pet owners.

There are some ALs that now allow small dogs and cats. Most ALs do not because of the trauma involved when an AL resident can no longer care for their pet (especially if the resident refuses to acknowledge that).

It is emotionally exhausting to convince a resident to rehome a pet, but it's unfair and uneconomical to expect staff members to take care of a resident's pet.

Typically, no SNF will allow resident pets. Either an AL or SNF, however, may include pet therapy with visits from well-trained, gentle dogs.

Ask to see the therapy rooms when you tour and see if they're busy and being managed in a professional way.

When are you allowed to tour?

There is no better way to test an AL or especially a SNF than by making unplanned, unannounced visits.

This does not mean showing up at midnight and expecting to be let in.

I mean visits during normal business hours and on weekends when management is not apt to be around.

If the facility will not let you visit, that should strike a loud warning bell.

Hopefully, while you're visiting, a resident will turn on a call light. Time how long it takes an employee to respond.

On the other hand, do not give too much credence to the architecture or furnishings.

Some poorly run SNFs look great because that's what relatives want to see when they are considering putting Mom or Dad there.

Buying nice furniture is a one-time cost while staffing with trained personnel is ongoing and expensive.

Facilities should be clean and comfortable, and that's it.

Did the facility pass the acid test?

The acid test is whether the facilities smell clean or not.

There may be an area where someone made a mess and it's not yet cleaned up but that bad odor should be a small, localized one, not the entire floor or facility.

Final comments on SNFs

If I haven't depressed you enough, this should do it. A 2013 Department of Health and Human Services study found that one in three people will die within their first year in a nursing home.

The SNF at my CCRC is very nice—for an SNF. One of the biggest problems is that Medicaid will not pay for private rooms and many, many people do not want to have to share a small room with a stranger—especially a stranger who may leave the television blasting full volume 24 hours a day.

My CCRC handled the room situation by having a dual wing structure. You enter one room but once through the door, there are a right and left area with a shared bathroom in the middle. That's as close to a private room as Medicaid will cover.

There is nothing pleasant about having to call for help to go the bathroom and if it happens to be at 2:30 a.m., no one may respond no matter how highly rated and expensive your SNF.

Memory Care

You may not be allowed to tour this part of the facility as it should be locked for the safety of the residents.

Take a hard look at the physical location and security arrangements.

Many residents with dementia tend to wonder around, and no facility you want to live in should enable residents to leave Memory Care and go outdoors by themselves.

The Washington Post newspaper did a 2024 series on accidental deaths at AL and SNF facilities, especially those that have been bought out by private equity groups (I hate private equity groups).

It was heartbreaking to read about a female dementia resident, wearing nothing but a nightgown, getting out of a facility at night and freezing to death because there was no way for her to get back in or contact facility personnel.

The growth in ownership by private equity groups began with a tax law change in 2008 that benefited equity groups, not residents.

From 2015 to 2019, more than 550 nursing homes that were certified by Medicare, Medicaid or both closed, according to LeadingAge, a trade association of non-profit senior care providers.

As of 2021, the Centers for Medicare and Medicaid Services estimated roughly 70 percent of nursing homes were for-profit facilities with 11% owned or controlled by private equity groups.

Definitely ask who owns the facility you're considering if it's not a non-profit and ask who manages it. There are companies that manage for-profit homes for their owners. This may be a positive check especially if the residence director is a former medical professional such as a nurse.

Ask about the programs the facility has for Memory Care residents. This is a complex illness that often requires diet changes, mobility support, physical therapy and trained staff that is sensitive to the emotional changes of residents.

Many dementia patients become agitated, angry and combative which is why so many are on various medications.

One final point. Memory Care facilities usually prefer that residents have private rooms (they need quiet places where they feel safe), but double rooms are less expensive.

If you have private insurance or participate in some government-funded program, you may not have a choice.

Sometimes family members will pay the difference between private and double rooms without it affecting the resident's ability to stay on the insurance or assistance plan.

Some facilities have walled-in outdoor patios that residents may use. All facilities will have some common areas. These may satisfy a resident's cabin fever.

Future improvements

There are initiatives aplenty to try to improve living conditions in AL and SNFs. One of the most popular is the concept of 'green homes.' There are more than 100 of these in 32 states.

Rather than large 100-bed facilities, green homes create less congested space with 10-12 residents to a house, each in a private room with bath, common space and dedicated CNA in the house. To date, these have been funded by private nonprofit organizations and foundations.

To what degree will these supplant institutional SNFs? Will Medicare and Medicaid fund private rooms? Don't wait until you need an SNF to find out. Lobby your federal representatives now to support these improvements.

Bottomline

Vote for office holders who support laws regulating ownership and operation of assisted living and skilled nursing facilities.

The current practice has a private equity group buying a facility, saddling it with debt, reducing operations and staff to save money and finally closing the facility when they've bled it dry – all the while benefiting from a tax code that makes many of the profits tax free.

Seven Tips to Make a Move Easier

Whether it's your own move or a family member's, the key point to remember is moving charges are based first on weight and then on distance.

Get rid of things—especially heavy things—before you move.

Hire a specialist in senior moves

This is far and away my favorite, albeit most expensive, tip. There are companies that specialize in moving seniors from their residences into retirement communities.

I hired one for a 92-year-old relative and the specialist arranged for the packing, moving and unpacking.

When my great-aunt walked into her retirement apartment, it was totally set up and ready to be lived in. What a relief for both of us.

The specialist was familiar with the retirement community, measured the rooms in the new apartment and drew up a floor plan.

She offered valuable guidance on what would be worth moving and what wouldn't fit in the new place. She showed great patience and kindness in helping my aunt navigate this move.

You can find these people at the National Association of Senior Move Managers **http://www.nasmm.org/**. Costs vary by location but typically range from $40 to $150 an hour.

Don't try to do everything at once

Most people recognize that their attic, garage or basement could use a good cleaning.

Start with one room a month. Do the attic, then the garage, then the basement.

Give away, throw away or sell items you don't want or haven't used in a year or could not use at the CCRC, such as snow shovels.

Once those areas are cleaned out, focus on groups of things such as clothing, dishes, tools or books.

If you're trying to help a relative get ready to move and they're reluctant, find a clothing drive or charity that is asking for donations.

Your mother might balk if you tell her she should get rid of her old clothes because she won't need them at the CCRC.

She might, however, be quite happy to help the church Boy Scout troop's rummage sale by donating all her old clothes.

Keep at it until you pare down to the things you need every day.

Take a hard look at your (or your family member's) furniture

I've lost count of how many people I've known who moved all their old stuff to their new home and then decided the old furniture was too big or too dark for their new, smaller independent living unit. What works in Milwaukee may not in Orlando.

Don't waste hundreds or even thousands of dollars moving furniture. Measure the rooms at your new home and then take a hard look at your existing furniture. Will it fit, both in terms of size and decor?

The most financially wasteful thing you can do is to move everything and then decide when you get there what you really want to keep.

Get quotes from three national companies if you're moving out of state

If you're moving within your city or state, the best way to find a moving company is through referrals from people you trust who've used the movers.

Otherwise, get written not-to-exceed quotes from the nationals. You'll see that some sweep through your home and quickly give you a not-to-exceed while others will take the time to see what you have and even open kitchen cabinets and closets.

Make sure you understand the conditions on the quote. Are there extra fees if your unit is upstairs, or the neighborhood doesn't allow 16-wheelers so they have to use smaller trucks, or if there's no driveway and they have to transport your items some distance? Is there a fuel surcharge?

Don't give the moving company a deposit. Make them bring the goods before they get any money from you.

Pack things yourself if you want to

Sometimes people have things they are afraid will be stolen so they pack them up themselves.

That's fine but then don't put on the outside of the box what it is. Just number your boxes, one to thirty or whatever.

Keep a list that only you have of all the contents in each numbered box.

If you box up an expensive thing(s) you know you want to keep and store in the box, write 'Baby Pictures' on it, and no one will steal it.

Consider pods

This is a newer concept whereby a company delivers a large container called a pod to your driveway. You pack it yourself. When it's ready, the company comes back and drives it to your new location.

Make sure you understand whether they deliver it to the company warehouse in your new city or directly to your new house. There may be additional charges for door-to-door delivery.

Also make sure you pack things very, very well. These pods do not have insulation or the same type of shock absorbers as national company moving vans so if your packed items can't stand some shaking, you may be unhappy with the results.

Deal with the carriers directly rather than through a broker

If you use the Internet, you'll be likely to wind up with a broker rather than a carrier.

These people take your information and then put your move out for quotes. You can get quotes yourself by contacting three of the national carriers directly.

Some Internet brokers also pay people to give them positive reviews so don't rely too heavily on feedback.

Few businesses get as many complaints as moving companies. Delays, stolen items and broken items are not uncommon.

Don't go with the lowest bid if it is significantly out of the range of the others.

You're asking for trouble by choosing a company based on price alone.

Bottomline

Get rid of as much stuff as you can (and all the heavy stuff) before you move.

Be realistic—moving is rarely trouble free, but a year later it will all be a vague memory.

Health Care and Insurance

Requirements

On the day you move in, expect to provide a copy of your Medicare and Medicare supplement insurance cards or other health insurance plans.

The CCRC also may ask for a copy of any Powers of Attorney (POAs) and medical directives you have such as a Do-Not-Resuscitate order or living will.

POAs enable another person to act on your behalf. The can be durable which means that the POA remains in effect even if you become incapacitated or mentally incompetent.

Ordinary or nondurable POAs expire if you become incompetent for whatever reason. These are usually for specific events such as letting a lawyer handle a divorce or a real estate agent handle your closing if you're out of the country.

All seniors would benefit by having a Medical Power of Attorney (POA) and Financial Power of Attorney. Both allow someone else to make medical or financial decisions for you if you are unable to do so.

Obviously, you want someone you trust to have these powers, and someone younger than you. Too many 80+ people pick a contemporary who often turns out to be as-much or even-more impaired than the subject of the POA.

It's worthwhile to have a lawyer or online law website, using the law of the state where your CCRC is located, draft POAs as well as your will or trust before you move in.

Medical insurance

Very few CCRCs are part of any Medicare Advantage Plan network. Very few insurance plans are interested in soliciting CCRCs with their limited number of beds for networks.

If you decide to enroll in an Advantage Plan, you need to run the numbers and understand how much you might have to pay to use your out-of-network CCRC for therapy or a nursing facility stay.

Consider this carefully. You can change from Advantage Plan to a Medigap supplement plan, but you may pay a higher premium than you would have if you had enrolled when you first eligible for Medicare Part B. The reverse, going from a Medigap to an Advantage Plan, usually does not raise your premium.

Run the numbers and consider your risks, both in overall health and potential for accidents, compared to what you might have to pay out of pocket.

Since this book was first published, a few CCRCs have formed their own Advantage Plans. This certainly makes health care convenient. Understand how easy or hard it would be to leave this plan if doesn't work out for you.

Medical staff

There are a few larger CCRCs that have on-site medical staff including a physician. One giant CCRC in Florida has five on-site physicians, all of whom handle only the CCRC residents.

At most facilities, you'll find a nurse onsite at normal business hours with provisions for 24/7 emergency calls.

Most CCRCs arrange for on-site physician visits from numerous specialties, such as a podiatrist, at regularly scheduled times.

One specialty that is usually overlooked is dental care. Many states won't allow mobile dental hygienists who could clean teeth and perform basic services, such as X-rays, for immobile seniors. See if your CCRC at least takes people to dental appointments.

There's nothing wrong with asking the CCRC director how the doctors are selected to come on site. Sometimes the doctors offer to come and sometimes the CCRC pays a fee for these visits. Other CCRCs charge the doctors a fee to use their facilities.

Every CCRC should offer transportation to doctor appointments at scheduled times. This is one of the advantages of living in a CCRC as opposed to having to rely on family, neighbors, or friends when you're not able to drive yourself.

Medicaid

Additionally, even if your CCRC is a Type A, your contract probably provides that you must apply for Medicaid to cover nursing facility costs if you can no longer afford private pay.

It's a good idea to have a Power of Attorney or a limited POA which would allow someone to establish a Miller trust (also called Qualified Income Trust or Income Only Trust) in case you become incapacitated for whatever reason.

Typically, people can't have a monthly income (2024 numbers) more than $2,829 for Medicaid to pay nursing home fees. If you are getting a pension and social security, you could find yourself receiving more than the Medicaid limit but not enough to cover the monthly cost of a nursing home.

The solution – if your state allows it – is to have a lawyer prepare a specific type of trust account known as Qualified Income, Income Only or Miller Trust. The monthly income that would disqualify you from Medicaid coverage goes into the trust fund.

Two caveats: 1) When you die, any funds in the trust account are given to the state Medicaid fund; and 2) not all pension providers are willing to have funds paid to a trust account. Social Security is always cooperative, however, so if the amount that puts you over the Medicaid limit is equal to your Social Security, have that placed in the trust.

Burial

Some CCRCs offer arrangements at an additional cost for burial or cremation. Many funeral homes offer prepaid cremation or burial plans.

I highly recommend making these arrangements in advance to ensure your wishes are carried out and to relieve family or friends of having to make difficult decisions.

Bottomline

It's getting harder to find primary care doctors will to take new Medicare patients and to find doctors that take any Medicaid patients. Get all the help from your CCRC you can.

Living Through the First Year

Regardless of which level of care you are at when you enter the CCRC, there will be a period of adjustment.

Give yourself at least six months before you decide you've made a terrible mistake.

It will be disorienting, and there will be periods of loneliness as you adjust to leaving a familiar homestead and living in a strange place where you may not know anyone else.

Living around so many other older people is a constant reminder of the effects of aging, such as not being able to drive at night or needing help to do something physically that you used to do yourself. Aging is just tough.

Here are some tips to help you adjust.

Eat at least one meal a day in the dining area until you make friends

I really appreciate CCRCs that assign seating. It's a good way to force residents to meet one another.

It's also a good way to minimize the cliques that form in any facility.

Attend resident council and management meetings

Show your interest in the community and your willingness to get involved.

Volunteer within the community

Call the volunteer coordinator or activities director and see what you can do to help out.

It may be as simple as helping hand out programs at a chapel service or as involved as teaching a craft class.

Join and participate

Bingo is an easy game to play and easy way to be around other people.

If you play bridge or pickleball, see if there are any groups at the CCRC. Even if they aren't taking on new members, these types of groups usually have a need for on-call, last-minute participants.

Most CCRCs have activities seven days a week, take part in as many as you can schedule.

Find the people and activities that click with you and then drop the ones that didn't resonate with you.

If you have a dog, walk him around the community

I met my best friends through my dog, both by dog walking together and at the community's dog park.

Don't be afraid to ask staff for help

You should have been assigned a staff member to help you with the move into the community. The CCRC also should have a process to file requests or complaints.

Many communities with a religious background have chaplains available, and they are an excellent source of support.

Bottomline

You won't make friends sitting home by yourself. If you're lonely at a CCRC, you have no one to blame but yourself.

Common Problems – Noise and People

Noise

If you're looking at apartment buildings where you'll be sharing walls and find one that looks like concrete blocks from the Stalin area, grab it.

These old buildings are infinitely quieter than today's stick-built ones.

The most frequent problem you'll have is loud television or music from next door.

After all, we all suffer some hearing loss as we age.

There isn't a senior community that hasn't had this problem and doesn't have a protocol to address it.

If this arises, ask the facilities manager for help.

Technology to the rescue

Often the solution will be special headphones or closed captioning television for your neighbor.

If you're a very light sleeper, you might use silicone ear plugs which do a good job of blocking noise.

Building problems

More difficult to solve are the results of poor construction. I've been in units where you could hear the neighbors talking, not to mention washing dishes and flushing toilets.

Soundproofing an apartment can be a complex undertaking and will require an experienced handyman or contractor. You'll also need management approval for most of the solutions.

Start with the easiest solution

People often think 'insulation' is the solution, and there are types of insulation that can be used in construction to block sounds.

The problem for current residents is that existing sheetrock would have to be removed to add insulation. This type of work becomes expensive rather quickly even if your management would even allow it.

An easier approach is to add a layer of sound-reduction drywall to your walls. You will lose an inch or so of space but this is a cost-effective way to minimize the sounds from your neighbor. An example of this is QuietRock at **http://www.quietrock.com/**.

The drywall won't address sound leaks from air ducting and electrical outlets or noise above and below you. As I said, noise reduction is a complex problem.

A good explanation is in this YouTube video from Mike Holmes of the TV show, Holmes on Homes: **http://youtu.be/ZlAZsYp2M-U.**

People

Learn to avoid some residents

In a senior community, there may be people who are in constant pain (example, severe arthritis) and are unintentionally cranky. The best policy is not to let their bad day become your day bad.

On the other hand, some seniors may be on the road to dementia, which could result in vile or even violent behavior.

Definitely avoid those people and report any threats or violent acts, no matter how seemingly mild, to a staff member.

Pushing someone or pulling something out of another resident's hand may not hurt the resident, but it is an act of violence that may be a precursor of worse behavior to come. Report it.

Be alert for people with a defined 'space' and stay away from it.

Better to let the man have his favorite chair than provoke a potentially violent tantrum.

Beware the bullies

If you ever dealt with high-school bullying, you'll recognize this in its senior form.

The best way to handle it is to confront attackers directly or to make jokes out of any would-be put downs.

If someone makes a snide comment about the way you're sitting, get up and ask them questions on the right way to sit.

Do I turn and put my rear to the seat first? Can I sit at an angle or straight back? Should I put the right hip first or the left? Should I cross my right leg? Should I swing my right foot? Be as sweet as you possibly can be.

A few minutes of this should dampen just about any bully's desire to provoke you.

Plus, no bully likes having someone else be the center of attention for too long.

Don't join in the gossip

Some communities seem more prone to this than others, but I've heard many residents at different communities complain that too many residents do nothing but gossip all day.

Bottomline

You can't avoid the normal problems associated with living closely to other people. It's a CCRC, not Fantasy Island.

Remedies When Things Go Wrong

If you're not happy about something at the CCRC, there may be some things you can do to set it right.

Try to resolve personnel issues at the lowest possible level

Depending on the issue, try to resolve problems with the individual or their supervisor. Continue up the chain of command to the Executive Director.

I've never heard of a staff/resident personnel problem that had to go beyond the Executive Director to be resolved.

If the problem is the Executive Director, take the matter up with the Board of Directors (but don't expect much).

Review the contract or CCRC rules

If the problem is a policy, review your contract to see if it details a grievance process.

Depending on the gravity of this issue, some contracts require, if your state allows it, mediation, or binding arbitration.

Instead of judges or juries, arbitrators decide if wrongdoing occurred and how to correct or compensate you for it.

Usually, the arbitrator's decision is final and can't be appealed in a court except under some very narrow circumstances.

Understand how much this process may cost you. If you lose, are you responsible for the other party's expenses?

There is no guarantee you will be successful, and it's worth remembering the old joke that 'arbitrator' is a combination of arbitrary and traitor.

See if the resident council can help

It's a plus if the CCRC has a residents' council (and some states require them) and at many CCRCs, one or two members of the residents' council become members of the CCRC's Board of Directors.

This is an excellent way to address policy issues.

The residents' council should also be a pathway for the families of residents to raise issues and concerns about the treatment of their family member or practices of the CCRC.

Some states have statewide groups that lobby on behalf of CCRC residents.

For example, the Florida Life Care Residents Association actively, and usually successfully, lobbies the Florida legislature and state agencies that regulate senior issues. It does not, however, address individual problems with a CCRC.

Consult an attorney

If you don't think your concern is being considered seriously, you can have a lawyer send the CCRC a letter explaining the problem.

That should get the Executive Director's attention, but understand that, once you take the problem outside of the community, you may cause some lingering bad feelings. Make sure your concern is important enough to risk this.

One of the most common causes for lawsuits by CCRC residents is the perceived misuse of entrance fees, particularly refundable fees.

One group of residents in an expensive for-profit community filed a class action lawsuit charging fraud after they found out the CCRC board members had used entrance fees to give themselves zero-interest 50-year loans rather than fund the life care trust the residents expected.

The case was settled out of the court, although residents did receive individual cash settlements and several improvements were made to the physical plant.

Some residents of CCRCs are retired accountants, lawyers and business people who understand how enterprises should be managed.

Few are hesitant to use the courts to enforce good management practices.

Contact the authorities

Although government action is usually associated with housing discrimination complaints, state and local agencies are—thankfully— becoming more willing to prosecute abuses.

They won't address personal gripes, but if you think the CCRC is engaging in unlawful or discriminatory acts, you can report them.

Bottomline

Residents always have the right to ask for changes but not all changes can be accommodated. You should at least be given a respectful and professional hearing.

Resources to Get You Started

Praise the Internet. It has never been easier to do your own research. Once you've decided where you want to live and the type of place you want, start searching.

Go to the **Medicare.gov** website and find out which CCRCs in your state of choice are certified for both Medicare and Medicaid. Their search tool is easy to use and will identify which communities are CCRCs.

If you want to further decrease the selection, you can use the search tool at CARF-CCAC (see below) for accredited ones. In my opinion, this is good for new CCRCs but not so important for long established ones.

Once you've narrowed the list, read the chapter on *Taking the Tour* and get ready to make your final choice.

Helpful websites

Commission on Accreditation of Rehabilitation Facilities and the Continuing Care Accreditation Commission (CARF-CCAC) - find accredited providers at **https://carf.org/find-provider/**.

Financial analysis

GuideStar at **http://www.guidestar.org/** has copies of many nonprofit IRS Form 990s and also offers individual detailed financial reports for a fee

LifeSite Logistics was started by a financial planner and an accountant, and offers financial data, such as occupancy rates, operating margins, and recent fee increases for hundreds of CCRCs at **https://mylifesite.net.** There also is a paid option if you want personalized data.

LeadingAge, formerly the American Association of Homes and Services for the Aging (AAHSA) - **http://www.leadingage.org/FindMember.aspx**

Medicare/Medicaid - find certified providers at **http://www.medicare.gov/NHCompare/Include/DataSection/Quest ions/ProximitySearch.asp**

National Long-Term Care Ombudsman Resource Center - find an independent advocate by state at **http://www.ltcombudsman.org/**

National Academy of Elder Law Attorneys - find an attorney who specializes in elder-care issues at **http://www.naela.org/**

Resident Associations

The National Continuing Care Residents Association (NaCCRA) has a website at **http://www.naccra.com** with some good information.

It's worth checking out to get the link to your state association, such as **Florida Life Care Residents Association (FLiCRA) http://www.flicra.com**, if one exists.

Benefits of Living in a CCRC

I've covered so many potential problems with CCRCs, you may have reached the end of this book and be wondering why you would even want to consider one.

There are real benefits to living in a CCRC:

- You don't have to try to look younger anymore. Lots of people stop coloring their hair (and I don't mean just women) and enjoy the many shades of gray in the community.
- You relieve your family from worrying about you, and you aren't a burden to them.
- You have the time and facilities to develop your talents or interests.
- You don't have to worry about, or perform your own home and yard maintenance.
- You can rely on the community for transportation if you're unable to drive or reach the point where you know you shouldn't be driving.
- You can travel anywhere, anytime without having to worry about your home.
- You can make friends with people in your own age group who share your frame of reference.
- You can develop a support group because your neighbors have the same type of problems you do and understand what you're going through.

- You're likely to receive better care in the AL, SNF or Memory Care because you already know many staff members there from your independent living days.
- You no longer have to wonder who'll take of you in your old age.

Bottomline

Nothing in life is perfect or guaranteed, but CCRCs have a good history of meeting resident needs. Just don't wait too long to make the move.

Example of Checklist for Your Tours

Here's an example to get you started. Subtract or add the items that are important to you. Just don't try to evaluate 200 things.

Item	Yes	No	Comment
Nonprofit operator			
Medicare and Medicaid certified nursing home			
Physical therapy on site			
Nearby medical facilities			
Signs staff is well treated and turnover is reasonable			
Garage is included in unit			
Dog friendly			
Washer/dryer or outlets in unit			
All electric appliances			
Thai food restaurants nearby			

Good Luck

The author is very open to suggestions on how to improve future editions of this guide. Please send comments/suggestions to **authorralvarez@gmail.com**.

If this book has been helpful, I would really appreciate it if you left a review – even a sentence or two is fine – at amazon.com **https://www.amazon.com/review/1480111805**.